Standardized Test Preparation for Language Arts

Teacher's Edition

Grade 2

Orlando   Boston   Dallas   Chicago   San Diego

Visit *The Learning Site!*
www.harcourtschool.com

Copyright © by Harcourt, Inc.

All rights reserved. No part of this publication may be reproduced or transmitted in any form or by any means, electronic or mechanical, including photocopy, recording, or any information storage and retrieval system, without permission in writing from the publisher.

Teachers using HARCOURT LANGUAGE may photocopy Copying Masters in complete pages in sufficient quantities for classroom use only and not for resale.

HARCOURT and the Harcourt Logo are trademarks of Harcourt, Inc.

Printed in the United States of America

ISBN 0-15-320250-5

6 7 8 9 10   073   2006 2005 2004

INTRODUCTION

This book prepares students for the language arts subtests of widely used achievement tests. At the Primary 2 level, these subtests are Listening, Language, Spelling, Word Study Skills, and Reading Vocabulary.

The student book is organized in the following three sections to lead students from scaffolded practice to independent performance.

1. **Modeled Instruction** This section explains each kind of test item. It includes skill-building lessons, models for choosing the answers to test items, and practice items with specific test-taking tips.

2. **Guided Practice** This is a practice section with tips related to specific items.

3. **Practice Test** This section simulates the actual test.

This Teacher's Edition begins with the **Directions for Administering**. The directions follow the order of the sections in the student book.

The Teacher's Edition also includes a **Student Profile** for recording students' scores as they progress through the book (see page T24). Use the chart below to help you plan administration of the **Practice Test**.

PRACTICE TEST PACING CHART

	Primary 2 End of grade 2; beginning of grade 3	Primary 3 End of grade 3; beginning of grade 4	Intermediate 1 End of grade 4; beginning of grade 5	Intermediate 2 End of grade 5; beginning of grade 6
Listening	38 items 30 mins	54 items 40 mins	40 items 30 mins	46 items 35 mins
Language	47 items 45 mins	74 items 70 mins	48 items 45 mins	38 items 35 mins
Study Skills			22 items 18 mins	22 items 18 mins
Spelling	30 items 25 mins	30 items 25 mins	20 items 15 mins	30 items 25 mins
Word Study Skills	32 items 18 mins			
Reading Vocabulary	22 items 15 mins	40 items 30 mins	30 items 20 mins	30 items 20 mins

Directions for Administering

USING THE STUDENT BOOK INTRODUCTION

The Student Book Introduction provides guidance for acquainting your students with standardized tests. Before students begin the work on page 9, guide them through the Student Book Introduction on pages 1–8.

Use with page 1.
Read the letter to the children. Ask them to describe how the tortoise and the hare are different. Have them tell some other things that the tortoise and the hare might do.

Use with pages 2–3.
Have students follow along as you read the paragraph in dark type and the tortoise's tips. Ask children to tell why being prepared will help them do better on a test. Read with children the directions for writing their names in the grid. Check to see that each child fills in the grid correctly.

Use with page 4.
Tell children that answer marking is an important test-taking skill. Explain that sometimes a machine will grade their tests, and they must mark each answer in the way that the machine will recognize it. Read the paragraph in dark type to children. Then help them complete the items on the page.

Use with page 5.
Describe to children what they should do when they see a sample item, a GO ON arrow, and a stop sign on a test. Then read the paragraph in dark type. Help children complete the items on the page.

Use with page 6.
Have students follow along as you read the paragraph in dark type. Show them how to do item 1. Then help them complete the items on the page.

Use with page 7.
Explain that there are different types of test pages and test questions. Read the tips aloud, and point out that they give steps in order. Have children complete the items on the page.

Use with page 8.
Read the checklist to children, and have them check the boxes to show what they will do when they take a test.

MODELED INSTRUCTION: LISTENING

Use with pages 9–10.

Read through the Modeled Instruction with students. Then read to them the sample item.

SAY **The giraffe nibbled leaves on the tree. *Nibbled* means the same as — *reached . . . ate . . . saw*. Which word means the same as *nibbled*?**

Have students work items 1–7 as you read each sentence.

1. **Look at the first group, Group 1. The breeze felt good on my skin. A *breeze* is —** *a light wind . . . hot sun . . . cold water.*

2. **Move to the next group of words, Group 2. The lake is still today. A *still* lake is —** *calm . . . deep . . . busy.*

3. **Move to the next group, Group 3. Which game did you decide to play? To *decide* something means to** *choose . . . take . . . act.*

4. **Look at the next group of words. The knock on the door surprised me. A *knock* is —** *a tap . . . paint . . . a sign.*

5. **Look at the next group of words. I hope Mom allows me to stay up late tonight. *Allows* means the same as —** *asks . . . meets . . . lets.*

6. **Look at the next group of words. Did you enjoy the book you read? To *enjoy* means to —** *hate . . . like . . . close.*

7. **Look at the next group of words. Going to the rain forest was quite an adventure. An *adventure* is —** *a long trip . . . a short trip . . . an exciting trip.*

Use with pages 11–12.
Read through the Modeled Instruction with students. Then read to them the sample story.

> Ann's father came home with a surprise in a big box.
>
> "What's in the box?" asked Ann. "Is it a computer?"
>
> "Guess again," Ann's father said.
>
> Just then, Ann heard a meow come from the box. "I know," she said. "It is a kitten!"

SAY Now I will ask you a question about the story. What did Ann's father bring home? Was it — *a computer . . . a doll . . .* or *a kitten*? Find the picture of what he brought home. Mark the space next to the picture.

Read the story for items 8 and 9.

> When Eric woke up, he could hear the rain beating against the window in his room. Sadly, he got out of bed and looked out the window anyway. "It has rained every day since my birthday," he said. "When will I ever get to ride my new bicycle?"

8. **Look at Row 8. How does Eric feel in this story? Does he feel —** *happy . . . sad . . .* or *scared*?

Directions

9   Now move down to the next row. Why couldn't Eric ride his bicycle? Was it because — *the bicycle had a flat tire . . . Eric had a broken leg . . .* or *it was raining*?

SAY   Now find the pictures beside number 10. Listen to the next paragraph. There will be one question.

> Koalas are interesting animals. They live in eucalyptus trees. Koalas sleep most of the day and are active mainly at night. Koalas eat young buds, leaves, and branches of the eucalyptus tree. Some people think koalas are bears, but they are not. Koalas are related to kangaroos.

10   Look at Row 10. Where do koalas live? Do they live in *a tree . . . a nest . . .* or *a den*?

Use with pages 13–14.
Read through the Modeled Instruction with students. Then read to them the sample paragraph.

> Not all baby animals look like their parents. A baby frog is called a tadpole. A tadpole looks more like a fish than a frog. It has a tail and no legs. It swims and breathes in the water. As the tadpole gets bigger, it grows legs and lungs. It loses its tail and gills. It can live and breathe on land. Now it looks like a frog!

SAY   Now listen to the question and the answer choices. What does an adult frog have that a baby frog does not have? Is it — *a tail . . . legs . . .* or *a tadpole*?

SAY   Find the section, right below the sample. Listen to this paragraph. There will be two questions.

> Here is a way to find out how much rain falls on a rainy day. Make a rain gauge. You will need a clear plastic container with a flat bottom, a ruler, and some tape. Tape the ruler onto the container. Then put the container outside. When the rain stops, look at the ruler to see how much rain fell in the container.

11   Look at number 11. What do you do after you tape the ruler onto the container? *Put the container outside . . . Look at the ruler . . . See the rain.*

12   Which of these is *not* something you need to make a rain gauge? *a plastic container with a flat bottom . . . a ruler . . . crayons.*

SAY   Now find the section with 13 through 15 in it. Listen to this paragraph. There will be three questions.

Directions

> Juan and his dad went to the circus. They held their breath as they watched men and women fly through the air on a trapeze. They laughed at the clowns. They watched in amazement as wild animals did tricks. "The circus was great fun," said Juan. "My favorite act was the man who rode a bicycle on the high wire."

13. The purpose of this paragraph is to — *give directions . . . give information . . . tell a story*.

14. Where does the story take place? *the beach . . . the zoo . . . the circus*.

15. What word describes how Juan felt at the circus? *excited . . . lonely . . . sad*.

SAY   Now find the section with 16 and 17 in it. Listen to this paragraph. There will be two questions.

> Animals have different ways to protect themselves from danger. Some animals, such as deer, have body coverings that blend in with their surroundings. This helps hide them from their enemies. Some animals, such as certain kinds of lizards, can change color to match their background. Other animals, such as turtles and porcupines, have body parts like hard shells or quills to protect themselves. Some animals can use their wings or legs to fly or run away from danger. A skunk can give off a strong odor that keeps its enemies away.

16. What is the main point of this story? *Animals have different body coverings. . . . Animals protect themselves in different ways. . . . Lizards can change color*.

17. How can a turtle protect itself? *By giving off a strong odor . . . By changing color . . . With its hard shell*.

MODELED INSTRUCTION: WORD STUDY SKILLS

Use with page 33.
Read through the Modeled Instruction with students. Have students work items 1 through 4 on their own.

Use with page 34.
Read through the Modeled Instruction with students. Have students find Sample B.

SAY   You see three words. Each word has a different ending. I will say one of the words and use it in a sentence. Then you will find the word. Mark under *writer*. You are a good *writer*. *Writer*.

SAY   Listen carefully to the word and sentence I say. Then mark the space under that word.

Directions

5. Mark under *running*. The school team is *running* in the race today. *Running*.

6. Go down to Row 6. Mark under *played*. Who *played* the winning team? *Played*.

7. Move down. Mark under *cleans*. Mariah *cleans* the spill on the floor. *Cleans*.

8. Go to the last row. Mark under *quickest*. Which runner is the *quickest*? *Quickest*.

Use with page 35.
Read through the Modeled Instruction with students. Then go over Sample C.

SAY Mark the space under the word that means *could not*. She *could not* finish her lunch.

9. Look at Row 9. Which one means *does not*? He *does not* like chocolate. *Does not*.

10. Go to Row 10. Which one means *we are*? *We are* going to buy new shoes. *We are*.

11. Move down. Which one means *were not*? The trees *were not* damaged in the storm. *Were not*.

Use with page 36.
Read through the Modeled Instruction with students. Discuss Sample D with students. Have students work items 12–16 on their own.

GUIDED PRACTICE: LISTENING

Use with page 41.

SAY I will read a sentence. Then I will say a word from the sentence and the three words that are written in your book as answer choices. One of the answer choices will mean the same thing as the word I say from the sentence. Choose that word and mark it in your book. Listen carefully.

1. Look at the first group, Group 1. Todd made himself a giant sandwich. *Giant* means the same as — small . . . jelly . . . huge.

2. Move down to the next group of words. The table is in the center of the room. The *center* of the room is the — middle . . . corner . . . doorway.

3. Dad is seldom sick. Seldom means — always . . . very . . . hardly ever.

4. Kim tries to imitate her big sister. To *imitate* means to — hurt . . . copy . . . hug.

5. Please lend me your pencil. To *lend* is to give . . . tell . . . write.

Use with page 42.

SAY I will read some stories and paragraphs to you. You need to listen carefully so you can answer some questions about them. The stories will have more than one question. I will read everything only once, so listen carefully and try to remember what I say.

SAY Find the section with 6 through 7 in it. Listen to this story. There will be two questions. The answers are pictures.

> Mother and Jen planted a garden. They planted beans, tomatoes, and cucumbers. They worked hard watering the plants and pulling the weeds. The plants grew quickly. One day Jen went out to the garden and saw that the first vegetables were ready to be picked. "Mother," she called with a big smile on her face. "The beans are ready to be picked. I'll get a basket to hold them all."

6 Look at Row 6, under the sample. What did Jen and her mother plant? Did they plant — *a garden . . . a flower . . .* or *a tree*?

7 Now move down to the next row. How did Jen feel when she saw the beans were ready? Did she feel — *sad . . . frightened . . .* or *happy*?

Use with page 43.

SAY In this part you will listen to more stories and paragraphs. Before reading each one, I will tell you the number of the questions for that story or paragraph. For each question I ask, I will also read the answer choices that are written in your book. The answers in this part are words or sentences. Listen to the answer choices. Choose your answer, and fill in the space next to it.

SAY Now find the section with 8 and 9 in it. Listen to this paragraph.

> What has wings and can fly but is not a bird? Did you guess a bat? If so, you are right. Bats may look like birds, but they are really mammals. Like other mammals, their bodies are covered with fur. They are the only mammals that can fly. Bats spend most of the day sleeping. They use the claws on their feet to hang upside down.

8 Look at number 8. What kind of animal is a bat? Is it a — *bird . . . mammal . . . fish*?

9 Look at number 9. Why do some people think bats are birds? *They have feathers . . . They have claws . . . They can fly.*

SAY Now find the section with 10 through 12 in it. Listen to this paragraph.

Directions

> Here is a way you can grow a plant. You will need a sweet potato, toothpicks, a plastic cup, and water. First put 4 or 5 toothpicks around the middle of the sweet potato. Then put the potato in the cup so that it balances on the rim. Add water to the cup until the bottom of the potato is covered. Check the water each day. Add more whenever you need to keep the bottom of the potato covered. After a while roots will grow into the water, and vines will sprout from the top of the potato.

10 The purpose of this paragraph is — *to give directions . . . to give information . . . to tell a story*.

11 What do you do after you put the potato in the cup? *Put in toothpicks . . . Cover the potato . . . Add water to the cup*.

12 What is a good name for this story? *Eating Sweet Potatoes . . . Planting Seeds . . . Growing Plants from Vegetables*.

GUIDED PRACTICE: WORD STUDY SKILLS

Use with pages 52–53.
Read the directions aloud to students. Then have them work items 1 through 4 on their own. Discuss their answers.

SAY **Now we will continue doing this activity. Put your finger on Row 5.**

Read the directions for items 5–8.

SAY **Listen carefully to the word and sentence I say. Then mark the space under that word.**

5 Mark under *talked*. Everyone *talked* at the same time. *Talked.*

6 Go down to Row 6. Mark under *slows*. The car *slows* to a stop. *Slows.*

7 Move down. Mark under *nicely*. The children sang *nicely* at the concert. *Nicely.*

8 Go to the last row. Mark under *smartest*. Sometimes the *smartest* players win the ball game. *Smartest.*

Read the directions for items 9–12.

SAY **In this activity, I will read two words and a sentence. You will mark under the shortened word in your booklet that means the same thing as the words I say.**

9 Which one means *she is*? *She is* looking for her jacket. *She is.*

10 Go to Row 10. Which one means *you will*? *You will* see the jacket in the closet. *You will.*

Directions

11   Move down. Which one means *I am*? *I am* going to wear this jacket. *I am*.

12   Go to Row 12. Which one means *cannot*? Mom *cannot* find her keys. *Cannot*.

After all children have finished marking their answer to Question 12, have them share and discuss their answers. Then read the next set of directions to children. Have them work items 13–15 on their own.

PRACTICE TEST: LISTENING

Use with pages 57–61.

It is especially important that you read the content of this subtest carefully and completely before reading it to the students. Be sure of all pronunciations.

For each passage, you will tell students how many questions there will be. Then read the passage. Read each question number before reading the question.

Read the test deliberately — not fast, but not slowly — and enunciate clearly. Do not repeat any passage or question unless instructions tell you to do so. Pause about 10 seconds between questions.

If you make a mistake in reading a question or direction, stop and say, "No. that is wrong. Listen again." Then read the question or direction correctly.

SAY **Look at the box with Sample A at the top of the page. I will read a sentence. Then I will say a word from the sentence and the three words that are written in your book as answer choices. One of the answer choices will mean the same thing as the word I say from the sentence. Choose that word and mark it in your book. Listen carefully.**

There was a clown at the party to entertain the children. To *entertain* means to *scare . . . amuse . . . help*. Which word means the same as *entertain*? Mark the space next to your answer.

SAY **Which space did you mark?**

Pause for replies.

SAY **Yes, you should have marked the space next to *amuse*, because to *amuse* means almost the same as to *entertain*. Does anyone have a question?**

SAY **Now we will continue. Listen carefully to what I say. Then mark the space next to your answer.**

1   **The newspaper is printed daily. *Daily* means — *every day . . . every week . . . every month*.**

2   **If you combine blue and yellow you will get green. To *combine* means to — *spill . . . use . . . mix*.**

3   **Melissa can recite the poem from memory. To *recite* is to — *whisper . . . repeat . . . sing*.**

4 The fierce wind blew down the tree. *Fierce* means — *warm . . . wild . . . calm.*

5 He grew weary as he walked up the mountain. *Weary* means — *angry . . . happy . . . tired.*

6 We saw a gigantic whale. *Gigantic* means — *very big . . . very old . . . very small.*

7 I cannot locate the missing book. To *locate* is to — *read . . . find . . . share.*

8 She is seldom sick. *Seldom* means — *always . . . not often . . . sometimes.*

9 He plays the music extremely loud. *Extremely* means — *very . . . hardly . . . mostly.*

10 The girl clutched her mother's hand. *Clutched* means — *shook . . . held tightly . . . waved.*

SAY Turn to page 58. This part of the test will also show how well you can listen. I will read some stories and paragraphs to you. You need to listen carefully so you can answer some questions about them. The stories will have more than one question. I will read everything only once, so listen carefully and try to remember what I say.

The answers in this part of the test are pictures. Look at Sample B at the top of the page. Look at the pictures. Listen carefully to the story and the question. Then mark the picture you think is right.

> "Lisa," called Mother, "Put on your sweater and come outside. You can help me rake the leaves."

Which picture shows what Lisa put on? Was it — *a hat . . . gloves . . .* or *a sweater*? Mark your answer.

SAY What space did you mark?

Pause for replies.

SAY Yes, that's right. You should have marked the space next to the sweater because Lisa's mother told her to put on a sweater.

Look at Sample C. Which picture shows what Lisa probably used to help her mother? Was it *a hammer . . . a rake . . .* or *a paintbrush*? Mark your answer.

SAY You should have marked the space next to the rake, because Lisa's mother asked her to help rake leaves. Does anyone have a question?

SAY Now we will do some more. Find the section with 11 and 12 in it. Listen to this paragraph. There will be two questions.

> When President Abraham Lincoln was a young boy, he lived in a log cabin. The cabin had a big fireplace inside. The fireplace was used for cooking. It helped keep the cabin warm. When it was dark, Lincoln read by the light from the fireplace.

11 What kind of house did young Abe Lincoln live in? Was it — *the White House* . . . *a tent* . . . or *a log cabin*?

12 What helped keep the cabin warm? Was it — *a blanket* . . . *a fireplace* . . . or *a stove*?

Now find the section with 13 and 14 in it. Listen to the next story. There will be two questions.

> What a fun morning Tom and Lee had at the pond! Snap, snap went their instant cameras. They took pictures of frogs, ducks, and birds. When they got home, they could hardly wait to show the pictures to Mom.
>   After Mom looked at all the pictures, Dad said, "I have a surprise for you. Come look in the van!"
>   They all went outside to the van. Dad took out a large bucket of water. "I scooped up some tadpoles," he said, "so you can watch them turn into frogs. Then we'll return to the pond and set them free!"
>   "Awesome," said Tom and Lee. "Thanks, Dad."

13 Where did Tom and Lee go in the morning? Did they go — *to school* . . . *to a pond* . . . or *to an airport*?

14 Which picture shows Dad's surprise? Was it — *a bucket with tadpoles in it* . . . *a puppy* . . . *a van*?

SAY Turn to page 59. For the next part of the test, you will listen to some more stories and paragraphs. For each question I ask, I will also read the answer choices that are written in your book. The answers in this part are words or sentences. Listen to the answer choices. Choose your answer and fill in the space next to it in your book. Let's try one for practice.

Find Sample D at the top of the page. Listen to this story, the question, and the answer choices that follow.

> Kevin took a table and chair outside on a hot summer day. He set them up on the lawn in front of his house. He put some cups and a pitcher of cold juice on the table. Then he taped a sign onto the table. It said, "Cold juice. 25¢ a cup." Before long, he had many customers. He had to go back into his house to get more juice.

Directions

Now listen to the question and the answer choices. What did Kevin sell? Did he sell — *milk* . . . *juice* . . . or *water*? Mark the space for your answer.

SAY Which answer did you choose? You should have marked the second answer, *juice*.

Find Sample E. Listen to the question and the answer choices. At what time of the year did this story take place? Did it take place in *winter* . . . *spring* . . . *summer* . . . or *fall*?

SAY Which answer did you choose? You should have marked the third answer, *summer*, because the story said it was a hot summer day. Are there any questions?

Answer any questions. Explain further if necessary.

SAY Now find the section with 15 through 17 in it. Listen to this paragraph. There will be three questions.

> What's your favorite way to eat ice cream? Many people like to eat ice cream cones. Some people think the ice cream cone was invented at the World's Fair in St. Louis, Missouri, in 1904. An ice-cream seller at the fair may have run out of plates on which to serve the ice cream. Since the seller's stand was next to a waffle stand, he rolled waffles and filled them with ice cream.

15 Where do people think ice-cream cones were invented? Was it — *in a park* . . . *at a fair* . . . *in a store*?

16 What does the word *stand* mean in this story? Does it mean — *a booth* . . . *the opposite of sit* . . . *a table*?

17 What is this story mostly about? *waffles* . . . *desserts* . . . *ice-cream cones*.

Now find the section with 18 through 20 in it. Listen to this paragraph. There will be three questions.

> Since we live close to the beach, we go there at night sometimes. Once we got to see a mother sea turtle lay her eggs in the dune. First she crawled out of the ocean and found a safe and quiet spot. Then she dug a small, but deep, hole for the eggs. We waited quietly in the dark until she finished and then watched her lay more than 100 eggs in the sand. Then when she was done, she covered up the hole and crawled back into the ocean.

18. Where do sea turtles lay their eggs? *on the beach . . . in the grass . . . in the ocean.*

19. What does the word *dune* mean in this story? *a small house . . . a hill in the sand . . . the ocean.*

20. How many eggs did the turtle lay? *100 . . . less than 100 . . . more than 100.*

SAY Now find the section with 21 through 23 in it. Listen to this paragraph. There will be three questions.

> Ice skating is a popular sport. Many people skate for fun and exercise. Some people enjoy figure skating. They perform movements such as leaps and spins as they move gracefully across the ice. Some people enjoy speed skating. They may compete in races. Skating was once an outdoor sport enjoyed in winter by people who lived where the weather is very cold. Today people can skate in all kinds of weather at indoor ice rinks.

21. This paragraph mainly tells — *how to figure skate . . . about different kinds of skating . . . where to find an ice rink . . . about skating races.*

22. The purpose of this paragraph is to — *give directions . . . tell a story . . . give information . . . explain how to ice skate.*

23. The paragraph mentions all these things about ice skating except — *people can skate indoors . . . skating is more popular than swimming . . . people can skate outdoors . . . people skate for fun.*

SAY Now find the section with 24 through 28 in it. Listen to this paragraph. There will be five questions.

> Here's a simple way to help feed the birds in your neighborhood. Make a bird feeder. You will need a clean, empty milk carton, scissors, string, and birdseed. First, get all the things you need. Next, cut an opening at the bottom of the milk carton. Then poke two holes through the side of the carton. Thread the string through the holes. Tie the string onto a tree branch to hang the feeder. Fill the bottom with birdseed, and watch the birds come to eat!

24. What is a good name for this story? *Watching Birds Eat . . . Making a Bird Feeder . . . An Art Project . . . Using Empty Milk Cartons.*

25. Which of these is not something you need to make a bird feeder? *milk carton . . . scissors . . . string . . . crayons.*

Directions

26 Does the person who wrote these directions think they are — *hard . . . easy . . . silly . . . long*?

27 What do you do after you poke holes through the side of the carton? *put a string through the holes . . . tie the string onto a tree branch . . . cut an opening in the bottom of the carton . . . put in birdseed.*

28 What is likely to happen after you hang your bird feeder? *It will fall down. . . . You tie a string onto it. . . . You will see birds come to eat. . . . You will be tired.*

SAY Now find the section with 29 and 30 in it. Listen to this paragraph. There will be two questions.

> Marisol took out a big mixing bowl. She put it on the table. Then she took out some flour, sugar, eggs, and butter. "All I need now is a mixing spoon," she said.

29 Why did Marisol probably take out the mixing bowl, flour, sugar, eggs, and butter? *She was hungry. . . . She was going to bake. . . . She was cleaning the closet. . . . She was going shopping.*

30 Where did Marisol put the mixing bowl? *in the sugar . . . on the floor . . . on the table . . . next to the spoon.*

Now find the section with 31 through 33 in it. Listen to this paragraph. There will be three questions.

> Every Wednesday afternoon, Paul and his mom go to the nursing home. They visit with some of the people who live there. Today, as soon as they arrived, Paul saw Mr. Green. They talked for a while about what Paul has been doing in school. Then Paul played a game of checkers with Mrs. Rose. As usual, Mrs. Rose won! As he was leaving, Paul waved to Mrs. Diaz. "Sorry we didn't have a chance to visit today," he said, "but I'll see you next week."

31 Which of these words would you use to describe Paul? *shy . . . rude . . . friendly . . . lazy.*

32 What did Paul do after he talked to Mr. Green? *waved to Mrs. Diaz . . . talked about school . . . left with his mother . . . played checkers.*

33 When do Paul and his mother visit the nursing home? *every day . . . Wednesday afternoons . . . once a month . . . Monday mornings.*

SAY Now find the section with 34 through 36 in it. Listen to this story. There will be four questions.

Directions

It had rained for days, but today the sun was out. Eric Hunter was entering Curly, his pet pig, in the 4-H event at the state fair.

"He'll win a ribbon," said his sister Wanda.

"I'm not so sure," said Eric as he placed Curly in a pen. "The judging won't take place until 4 o'clock. Curly is too frisky to stay caged up for a long time."

"We'll wait here with Curly." said Mr. Hunter. "You go have some fun."

Eric and Wanda headed to the Ferris wheel. Up they went. They could see the whole fair. Then Eric spotted a pig running.

"Isn't that Curly?" he asked. "How could Curly be out of his pen?"

When the ride was over, Eric and Wanda rushed to the pig barn. "Where is Curly?" he asked with tears running down his cheeks.

"A little boy opened the gate and Curly just ran out," said Mrs. Hunter. "Don't worry. We'll find him."

Eric and Wanda looked near the roller coaster. They looked around the hot dog stand. They looked near the Bingo game.

"Look," shouted Wanda. "Aren't those pig footprints? Let's follow them."

Eric and Wanda followed the footprints. There was Curly in a puddle of water behind the refreshment stand. "Well, well," said Wanda. "I guess Curly would rather take a cool bath than win a ribbon."

34 What kind of animal is Curly? *a dog . . . a cat . . . a horse . . . a pig.*

35 How did Eric feel when he saw that Curly got out of the pen? *happy . . . sad . . . angry . . . excited.*

36 Where did Eric and Wanda find Curly? *by the ferris wheel . . . by the roller coaster . . . by the refreshment stand . . . by the Bingo game.*

Now find the section with 37 and 38 in it. Listen to this paragraph. There will be two questions.

Your body is full of muscles. They help make other parts of your body move. Most muscles move bones, which let you do things such as walk, run, or throw a ball. Some muscles move parts of your body that are not bones, such as your heart. There are more than 600 muscles in your body. It takes about 43 muscles to frown. But it only takes 17 muscles to smile!

37 What part of your body helps you move? *bones . . . muscles . . . heart . . . legs.*

38 According to the paragraph, about how many muscles does it take to smile? *600 . . . 50 . . . 43 . . . 17.*

Directions

PRACTICE TEST: LANGUAGE

Use with pages 62–64.

SAY In this activity, I will read a sentence and then I will ask a question about it. Look at Sample A. Listen carefully. *"Have you seen my <u>book</u>."*

How should the underlined part be written? Should it be *Book!* with a capital "B" and an exclamation point, like the first answer choice; *book?* with a small "b" and a question mark, like the second answer choice; or should it be written *The way it is?* Listen to the sentence again. *"Have you seen my book?"* What is the answer?

Pause for replies.

SAY Yes, that's right. The second answer is the correct way to write the underlined part of this sentence. The sentence is a question, and "book" should not be capitalized. The space for the second answer has been filled in to show that it is the correct answer. Does everyone understand why the second answer is the correct one?

SAY Now move down to the next box, Sample B. Listen carefully. *"That kitten <u>is</u> very cute."* How should the underlined word be written?

Should it be *are, were*, or should it be written *The way it is*? Mark the space next to your answer.

Which space did you mark?

Pause for replies.

SAY Yes, that's right. You should have marked the space for the third answer, because the underlined word in this sentence should be written *The way it is.* "That kitten is very cute" is correct, isn't it? If you did not mark the correct answer, erase your first mark and mark the third answer now. Does everyone understand this activity?

Answer any questions. Explain further if necessary.

SAY Now we will continue doing this activity. Put your finger on number 1, right under Sample B. *"Would you like a clean towel, aunt Julie?"* How should the underlined part be written? Look closely at the punctuation and capitalization, and then mark your answer.

Continue in this manner for items 2–20. Read the sentences and the answer choices aloud.

Use with pages 64–66.

SAY Look at the group of words in the box. Read them to yourself as I read them aloud. *"The bird flew. Up in the tree."* How should this group of words be written to make a complete and correct sentence? Should it be written *The bird flying up in the tree. ...The bird flew up in the tree. ...* or is this a complete and correct sentence *The way it is*?

Directions

Pause for replies.

SAY **Yes, that is correct. The second group of words, *The bird flew up in the tree*, is a complete and correct sentence. Does everyone understand what we just did?**

SAY **Now look at Sample D. Read the group of words in the box to yourself as I read it aloud:** *"Nan played with her toy drum."* **How should this group of words be written to make a complete and correct sentence? Look at the answer choices. Should the group of words in the box be written *Nan playing with her toy drum*. like the first answer choice; *Nan played. With her toy drum*. like the second answer choice; or should it be written *The way it is*? Mark the space next to your answer.**

Which answer did you mark?

Pause for replies.

SAY **You should have marked the third answer because *"Nan played with her toy drum"* is a complete and correct sentence *The way it is*. Does everyone understand how to do this activity?**

Answer any questions. Explain further if necessary.

SAY **Now we will continue doing this activity. Put your finger on Box 21, right under Sample D.** *"Mr. Rodgers raking the front lawn."* **How should the group of words in the box be written? Should it be written *Mr. Rodgers rakes the front lawn*. like the first answer choice; *Mr. Rodgers. He rakes the front lawn*. like the second answer choice; or should it be written *The way it is*? Mark your answer.**

Give children about 10 seconds to answer Question 21.

Continue in this manner for questions 22–33, reading all sentences and answer choices aloud.

Use with pages 67–69.

SAY **Put your finger on the word Sample at the top of page 67. Here you see a story. After the story, there are two questions. Follow along as I read the story aloud.**

Read the sample story to students.

SAY **Now read Question E to yourself as I read it aloud.** *"Which of these would go best after the last sentence? Ann's uncle has a big apple tree beside his house. ...An apple makes a great after-school snack. ...Next time you buy apples, look at all the different kinds!"* **What is the answer?**

Pause for replies.

SAY **Yes, that's right. The story is about different kinds of apples, so the**

Directions
T19

correct answer is *Next time you buy apples, look at all the different kinds!* Does anyone have a question?

SAY **Now we will look at Question F. Read Question F to yourself as I read it aloud. Mark the space next to the answer you think is right.**

SAY **Which space did you mark?**

Pause for replies.

SAY **Yes, you should have marked the space next to the second answer, because the story *tells about types of apples*. Does everyone understand what we just did?**

Answer any questions. Explain further if necessary.

SAY **Find Story 1 underneath Sample F. Read the story to yourself as I read it aloud.**

Read the story and the questions and answer choices aloud. Give students time to mark their answers. Continue in this manner with Stories 2, 3, and 4.

Begin the activity for Sample G.

SAY **Look at the words in the box: *inch . . . know . . . hawk*. Which word comes first in A-B-C order? Is it *inch, know,* or *hawk*? Mark the space next to your answer. You should have marked the space next to *hawk* because *hawk* comes first in A-B-C order. Now we will continue doing this activity. Listen carefully to what I say. Then mark the space next to the word you think is right.**

44 **Which word comes first in alphabetical (A-B-C) order? Is it *table, seahorse,* or *umbrella*?**

45 **Which word comes first in alphabetical (A-B-C) order? Is it *city, chore,* or *close*?**

46 **Which word comes first in alphabetical (A-B-C) order? Is it *mild, price,* or *medicine*?**

47 **Which word comes first in alphabetical (A-B-C) order? Is it *nurse, lift,* or *mail*?**

PRACTICE TEST: SPELLING

Use with pages 71–73.

SAY **Find the sample in the shaded box at the top of page 71. Here you see four sentences. A word is underlined in each sentence. One of the underlined words is spelled incorrectly. Which one is it? Mark the space next to your answer.**

SAY **Which space did you mark?**

Pause for replies.

SAY **Yes, that's right. In the third sentence, the word *crowd* is not spelled correctly. It should be spelled *c-r-o-w-d,* not *c-r-o-u-d.* You should have marked the space next to the third sentence. Are there any questions?**

SAY **You will do the rest of the questions on this page and the next two pages on your own. Keep working until you come to the stop sign.**

PRACTICE TEST: WORD STUDY SKILLS

Use with pages 74–75.

SAY **Look at Sample A in the shaded box at the top of the page. Here you see the words *player . . . sunshine . . . uncover.* Which one of these words has two words in it?**

Pause for replies.

SAY **Yes, that's right. *Sunshine* is made up of two words—*sun* and *shine.* Does anyone have a question?**

Answer any questions the children may have. Repeat Sample A if necessary.

SAY **You will do the next four rows by yourself. Work until you come to the next shaded box. Then put your pencil down and wait. Remember, find the word that is made up of two words and mark the space under it. Stop when you come to the shaded box. Are there any questions?**

SAY **Now put your finger on Row 1, right below Sample A. Start working.**

While children are working, walk around the room to make sure they are following directions, but give no help on specific questions.

SAY **Now put your finger on Sample B in the shaded box that is in the middle of the column. You see three words. These words look a lot alike, but they have different endings. I will say one of these words and use it in a sentence. Then you will find the word. Listen carefully.**

Which is the word *sweetest*? Tutti Frutti is the *sweetest* ice cream. *Sweetest.*

SAY **You should have marked the space under the third word because it is the word *sweetest.* Raise your hand if you have a question.**

Answer the students' questions.

SAY **Now we will continue doing this activity. Put your finger on Row 5, right under Sample B. Listen carefully to the word and sentence I say. Then mark the space under that word.**

5 **Mark under *brushed.* Grandpa *brushed* the dogs. *Brushed.***

Directions

6   Go down to Row 6. Mark under *covering*. Dad is *covering* the plants so they won't freeze. *Covering*.

7   Move down. Mark under *builder*. Who is the *builder* for this house? *Builder*.

8   Go to the last row. Mark under *shortly*. We can leave the meeting *shortly*. *Shortly*.

SAY   Stop. Put your pencil down. Put your finger on Sample C in the shaded box at the top of the next column. In Sample C you see the words *hasn't . . . haven't . . . wasn't*. Each of these words is a shortened form of two other words. Each shortened form has the same meaning as the two words it comes from. I will say the two words and use them in a sentence. Then you will find the shortened word that means the same and mark under it. Listen carefully. Mark the space under the word that means *have not*. I *have not* seen my cat today. *Have not*.

Which space did you mark?

Pause for replies.

SAY   Yes, that's right. You should have marked the space under the second word, *haven't*, because it has the same meaning as *have not*. Does anyone have a question?

SAY   Now put your finger on Row 9, right under Sample C. We will continue doing this activity. Listen carefully to the two words and the sentence I say. Then mark under the shortened word in your booklet that means the same thing as the words I say.

Read each question. Pause about 10 seconds between questions.

SAY

9   Look at Row 9. Which one means *you have*? *You have* got a new puppy! *You have*.

10   Go to Row 10. Which one means *that is*? *That is* a very cute puppy. *That is*.

11   Move down. Which one means *we will*? *We will* wait for you here. *We will*.

12   Go to Row 12. Which one means *is not*? The baby *is not* crying. *Is not*.

SAY   Stop. Put your pencil down. Put your finger on Sample D under Row 12. In Sample D you see four words. The first word is *jet*. The letter *j* in *jet* has a line under it. Think of the sound of the letter *j* in *jet*. Look at the other three words in the row. Which word has the same /j/ sound as the letter *j* in *jet*?

Pause for replies.

SAY **Yes, that's right. Edge has the same /j/ sound as *jet,* so you should mark the space under the word *edge* to show that it is the right answer. Does anyone have a question?**

SAY **You will do all the rows like this on your own. In each row, look at the first word and say it quietly to yourself. Listen for the sound or sounds that are made by the letter or letters that have lines under them. Then say the other three words in the row quietly to yourself and find the word that has the same sound or sounds as the underlined letter or letters in the first word.**

When you come to the bottom of page 75, where you see the stop sign, put your pencil down. You may check your work on pages 74–75, but do not look at any other pages. Does anyone have a question?

Answer the students' questions. Repeat instructions if necessary.

While the students are working, walk quietly about the room to make sure they are following directions, but do not give help on specific questions.

PRACTICE TEST: READING VOCABULARY

Use with pages 76–78.

SAY **Find the sample in the shaded box at the top of page 76. You will choose the word that means the same, or about the same, as the underlined word. *A tale is a kind of — toy . . . game . . . story . . . picture.* Mark the space next to the word that means the same, or about the same, as the underlined word, *tale.***

SAY **What space did you mark?**

Pause for replies.

SAY **Yes, that's right. You should have marked the space next to *story,* because *story* means about the same as *tale.* Does anyone have a question?**

Have students work on their own to complete items 1–12.

Guide students through Sample B at the top of page 77, and have them work on their own to complete items 13–16.

Guide students through Sample C on page 78, and have them work on their own to complete items 17–22.

Student Profile

Student's Name _____

Teacher's Name _____

SUBTESTS	Date/Score Modeled Instruction	Date/Score Guided Practice	Date/Score Practice Test
Listening 1. vocabulary 2. comprehension			
Language 1. mechanics and usage 2. sentence structure 3. expression (content, organization) 4. A-B-C order			
Spelling 1. sight words 2. phonetic principles (consonant sounds, vowel sounds) 3. structural principles (inflections)			
Word Study Skills 1. structural analysis (compounds, inflections, contractions) 2. phonetic analysis—consonants (single, clusters, digraphs) 3. phonetic analysis—vowels (short, long, other)			
Reading Vocabulary 1. synonyms 2. multiple-meaning words 3. context			

Strengths/Areas for Improvement: _____

_____

_____

_____

Standardized Test Preparation for Language Arts

Student Edition

Grade 2

Orlando   Boston   Dallas   Chicago   San Diego

Visit *The Learning Site!*
www.harcourtschool.com

Copyright © by Harcourt, Inc.

All rights reserved. No part of this publication may be reproduced or transmitted in any form or by any means, electronic or mechanical, including photocopy, recording, or any information storage and retrieval system, without permission in writing from the publisher.

Requests for permission to make copies of any part of the work should be mailed to the following address: School Permissions, Harcourt, Inc., 6277 Sea Harbor Drive, Orlando, Florida 32887-6777.

HARCOURT and the Harcourt Logo are trademarks of Harcourt, Inc.

Printed in the United States of America

ISBN 0-15-321223-3

6 7 8 9 10   073   2006 2005 2004

Contents

Introduction 1

Modeled Instruction
Listening 9
Language 15
Spelling 29
Word Study Skills 33
Reading Vocabulary 37

Guided Practice
Listening 41
Language 44
Spelling 50
Word Study Skills 52
Reading Vocabulary 54

Practice Test
Listening 57
Language 62
Spelling 71
Word Study Skills 74
Reading Vocabulary 76

Dear Student,

    Once a year the children in your school take a special test. This test helps the teachers and the principal know what you are learning.

    Taking the test is easier when you know how. This book will help you learn how. It will give you practice listening carefully, reading carefully, and following directions.

    Take some hints from the tortoise and the hare. The tortoise reads carefully and chooses the best answers. The hare is careless and makes mistakes. Which one will you be like?

Will you be the tortoise or the hare?

"I didn't listen to the directions."

"I filled in the wrong circle."

"I didn't read carefully."

- **LISTEN** carefully.
- **READ** carefully.
- **CHOOSE** the best answer.
- **MARK** answer choices carefully.
- **CHECK** your work.

Introduction

Name _____

Getting Prepared

The tortoise is always prepared and ready to pay attention to the teacher. Think about how you can be ready for a test. Then read the tortoise's tips below.

Tips for Listening

 1. Sit quietly.
 2. Look at the speaker.
 3. Listen for directions.
 4. Do not pay attention to other students.

Tips for Taking a Test

1. Sit up straight in your chair.
2. Keep your eyes on the teacher or on the test booklet.
3. Have your sharpened pencils ready.

Will you be the tortoise or the hare?

Name _____

Writing Your Name

Before you take a test, you will fill in information on a grid that looks similar to the one below. Follow the directions to write your first name in the grid.

1. Print your first name, putting just one letter in each white box.

2. Below each box, fill in the circle that has the same letter you wrote.

3. For each box that you did not write a letter, fill in the empty circle at the top of the column.

Introduction

Name _____

Answer Marking

You should mark answer choices carefully when you take a test. The tortoise fills each circle completely. The hare is messy and marks outside the circle. Follow the directions for each item below. Mark your answers as the tortoise would.

1 Mark the answer circle on the left.

2 Mark the answer circle on the right.

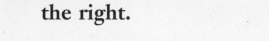

3 Mark the answer circle at the top.

4 Mark the answer circle at the bottom.

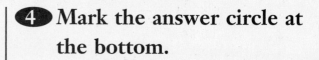

5 Mark the answer circle for the picture of the hare.

6 Mark the answer circle for the picture of the tortoise.

Introduction

Name _____

Important Words

You will see some important words when you take tests. These words tell you what to do. Look at the words and pictures. Then answer the questions. Remember to mark your answer choice as tortoise would.

1 What word or words tell you to keep working?

2 What word or words tell you the teacher will show you how to do an item?

3 What word or words tell you to put your pencil down?

Introduction

Name _____

Important Information

Sometimes important information on a test has a line under it. Sometimes the information is in a box. The hare gets questions wrong because he does not pay attention to the important information. Look at each of the items below. Mark the answer circle that shows the important information from the question.

1 m<u>u</u>g

    m   **u**   g

2 b<u>o</u>at

    b   **oa**   t

3 dri<u>nk</u>

    dr   i   **nk**

4 Something that is <u>untied</u> is _____.

    that is   **untied**   Something

5 Which one tells something Kenny did <u>not</u> do?

    Kenny   tells   **not**

6 What is the <u>best</u> title for this story?

    best   title   story

7 Who is ready to <u>play</u>?

    Who   is   **play?**

Introduction

Name _____

Test-Taking Tips

Sometimes you will read a story as your teacher reads it aloud. Then you will answer questions about the story. Look at page 67 in this book. It shows an example of this kind of test page. Use the tortoise's tips and the test page to answer the questions below.

 Read along with your teacher.

 Think about the meaning of the story.

 Read along as your teacher reads each question and the answer choices.

☑ Look back at the story to see which answer is best.

1 What does this test page show?

○ Rows of words
● A story and questions
○ A group of words and questions

2 What should you do while reading this story?

○ Think about the meaning of the story.
○ Think about other stories you have read.
○ Look at the questions.

3 What is the best way to choose the answer to a question?

○ Use your own ideas.
○ Guess.
● Check the answer with the story.

Name _____

I will
- ☐ listen carefully
- ☐ read carefully
- ☐ follow directions
- ☐ mark answers carefully
- ☐ begin where told
- ☐ begin when told
- ☐ stop when told
- ☐ guess carefully
- ☐ check my answers
- ☐ pay attention only to the teacher and the test
- ☐ do the best I can

Name _____

Modeled Instruction: Listening

This part of the test will check how well you can listen. The first activity is about the meaning of words. Your teacher will say a sentence and then ask you what one of the words means.

Listening Skills Good listeners pay attention to the speaker. You will be able to listen better if you look at your teacher as he or she speaks. Think about what your teacher is saying. Do not look out the window or daydream.

Test-Taking Tip Try to remember the sentence as your teacher reads the answer choices. Think of which answer means the same thing as the word in the sentence.

Use the Sample In the sentence your teacher read, *nibbled* means the same as *ate*. Mark the space next to *ate*.

> **SAMPLE**
> ○ reached
> ○ ate
> ○ saw

Practice

Listening

DIRECTIONS
Listen as your teacher reads a sentence and then asks about one word from the sentence. Choose the meaning of that word. Mark the space next to your answer.

1 ● a light wind
○ hot sun
○ cold water

Modeled Instruction
9

Name _____

2
- ○ calm
- ○ deep
- ○ busy

3
- ○ choose
- ○ take
- ○ act

4
- ○ paint
- ○ tap
- ○ sign

5
- ○ asks
- ○ meets
- ○ lets

6
- ○ hate
- ○ like
- ○ close

7
- ○ a long trip
- ○ a short trip
- ○ an exciting trip

Tip
Have you heard the word *still* before? What did it mean? Choose the word that means the same as *still* and makes sense in this sentence.

Tip
Think about what the word *knock* means. Is a knock on the door something you see or hear? Which word choice names something you can hear?

Tip
Think about what the word *enjoy* means. Think of something you enjoy. Is it something you hate, like, or close? Choose the word that is closest in meaning to *enjoy*.

Name _____

Modeled Instruction: Listening

Listening Skills	In the next activity, you will listen to stories and paragraphs. Then you will answer questions about them. The answers in this part of the test are pictures. You will choose the picture that best shows the answer to each question.
	When a story is read, you should listen for the answers to some questions: Who or what is the story about? When and where does the story take place? What happens to the characters in the story?
Test-Taking Tip	Make pictures in your mind as you listen to the story. That will help you know which picture is the right answer choice.
Use the Sample	Here is an example of what you will be hearing on the test. Listen carefully. Then answer the question.
	When you listened, you heard that Ann's father brought home a surprise in a box. First, Ann guessed that the surprise was a computer. Then she heard a meow come from the box and she knew it was a kitten. The picture of the kitten is the right answer.

Modeled Instruction

Name _____

Practice

Listening

8 ○
●
○

9 ○
○
●

> **Tip**
> There could be many reasons why someone couldn't ride a bicycle. Make sure you choose the picture that shows the reason that was in the story.

10 ●
○
○

Modeled Instruction

Name _____

Modeled Instruction: Listening

In this last listening activity, you will listen to stories and paragraphs. Then you will answer questions about them. The answers are words or sentences.

Listening Skills
As you listen, try to keep track of the main point of what you hear. If you are listening to a story, think about what happens. If you are listening to instructions, think about the order of the steps. If the paragraph gives information, listen for the main facts.

Use the Sample
Here is an example of what you will be hearing on the test. Listen carefully. Then answer the question.

Making a picture in your mind could help you remember that a tadpole has a tail and no legs. Since adult frogs do have legs, <u>legs</u> is the right answer. Frogs have legs; tadpoles do not.

SAMPLE
○ a tail
● legs
○ a tadpole

Practice

Listening

DIRECTIONS
Listen as your teacher reads a paragraph. Then listen to each question about the paragraph. Choose the best answer.

11 ● Put the container outside.
○ Look at the ruler.
○ See the rain.

Modeled Instruction
13

Name _____

12
○ a plastic container with a flat bottom
○ a ruler
● crayons

> 💡 **Tip**
> Notice that this question asks what you do **not** need. Think about the directions. Mark the answer that is **not** mentioned in the paragraph.

13
○ give directions
○ give information
● tell a story

14
○ the beach
○ the zoo
● the circus

15
● excited
○ lonely
○ sad

> 💡 **Tip**
> Some stories give you clues about the way people feel. In this story you heard that Juan held his breath, laughed, and watched the circus in amazement. Which answer best describes how he felt, based on these clues?

16
○ Animals have different body coverings.
● Animals protect themselves in different ways.
○ Lizards can change color.

> 💡 **Tip**
> All three answer choices are mentioned in the paragraph, but only one choice is the <u>main idea</u> of the paragraph. The other choices are details that support that idea.

17
○ By giving off a strong odor
○ By changing color
● With its hard shell

Modeled Instruction

Name _____

Modeled Instruction: Language

This part of the test is about using language. The first activity has two kinds of questions:

- questions about using capital letters and punctuation marks
- questions about using verbs

Capitalization Use capital letters for special nouns that name people, places, or things. You should also capitalize the first word in a sentence.

Punctuation This chart shows the main punctuation rules that you need to know for the test.

period (.)	at the end of a telling sentence
question mark (?)	at the end of an asking sentence
exclamation point (!)	at the end of an exclaiming sentence
comma (,)	between city and state (Orlando, Florida)
	after letter parts (Your friend,)
apostrophe (')	in contractions (I'm coming.)

Test-Taking Tip You will check the correctness of the underlined part for each item. If there is a mistake, ask yourself how you would fix it. Look at the answer choices to see if any match your ideas.

Read the Sample When you read the whole sentence, you know it asks a question. This means it must end with a question mark. Only one answer choice has this punctuation mark.

> **SAMPLE**
> Where will we play <u>today.</u>
>
> ○ Today
>
> ○ today?
>
> ○ The way it is

Modeled Instruction

Name

Practice

Language

DIRECTIONS
Choose the word or group of words that tells how the underlined part of the sentence should be written. If there is no mistake in the underlined part, choose *The way it is*.

1 What is the best way to write this beginning of a letter?
<u>Dear Sam</u>

- ○ dear Sam
- ◉ Dear Sam,
- ○ The way it is

Tip
Think about friendly letters you have written. The greeting always begins with a capital letter. The name is always followed by a comma.

2 I went to the <u>store with Mark.</u>

- ○ Store with Mark.
- ○ store with mark.
- ○ The way it is

Tip
Think about the rules you know for capital letters. The word *store* does not name a special store. Does *Mark* name a person?

3 On <u>monday we didn't</u> have music.

- ○ monday we didnt
- ◉ Monday we didn't
- ○ The way it is

4 I don't like the story "<u>Tall trees.</u>"

- ○ "Tall Trees."
- ○ "tall trees"
- ○ The way it is

Tip
Remember that all the important words in a story title need to begin with a capital letter. All the answer choices have quotation marks.

Modeled Instruction
16

Name

5 The game will be played at <u>Hillside Park.</u>
- ○ Hillside park.
- ○ Hillside Park?
- ● The way it is

> **Tip**
> Remember, these questions are about punctuation marks and capital letters. If you don't see a problem right away, check for each of these problems.

6 Let's go to the <u>movies?</u>
- ○ Movies
- ● movies.
- ○ The way it is

> **Tip**
> Ask yourself if this is a telling sentence or an asking sentence.

7 We took a trip to <u>Columbus Ohio.</u>
- ● Columbus, Ohio.
- ○ columbus, ohio.
- ○ The way it is

> **Tip**
> How do you write the names of a city and a state? Should a comma come between them? What capital letters are needed?

8 My birthday this year is <u>Wednesday July 4.</u>
- ○ wednesday July 4.
- ● Wednesday, July 4.
- ○ The way it is

9 What a wonderful <u>time we had!</u>
- ○ time we had?
- ○ Time we had?
- ● The way it is

Modeled Instruction
17

GO ON

Modeled Instruction: Language

Using Verbs Some of the questions in this part will check to see if you know the correct form of an action word or verb. Read this sentence:

> **My grandfather taked us to the movies.**

This sentence does not sound the way you would say it. You would check to see if the word *took* is one of the answer choices.

Test-Taking Tip To tell whether a sentence part is correct, be sure to read and think about the whole sentence.

Other questions have sentences with more than one verb. Check to see if both verbs work together. Here is an example:

> **She felt so sad when her friend moves.**

Since the verb *felt* tells about the past, the verb *moves* should be changed to *moved*.

Read the Sample The underlined part sounds correct because it is correct. Choose the answer *The way it is*.

SAMPLE
We slept late yesterday morning.

○ We sleep

○ We sleeped

○ The way it is

Name _____

Practice

Language

10 He <u>throw</u> the ball and made an out.
- ○ throwed
- ◉ threw
- ○ The way it is

Tip
There are two verbs in this sentence, and both need to tell about the same time. Ask yourself what form of *throw* you use to tell about the past.

11 The <u>child play</u> in the park.
- ◉ child plays
- ○ child are playing
- ○ The way it is

Tip
Think about the way subjects and verbs go together. The word *child* tells about one person. Choose the verb form that sounds right when the subject names just one.

12 It is so funny when the baby <u>makes</u> silly faces.
- ○ was making
- ○ made
- ◉ The way it is

Tip
Start by looking at the two verbs in this sentence. The word *is* gives you a clue that something is happening now. Make sure that the other verb describes something that is also happening in the present.

13 We are going inside because it <u>was raining.</u>
- ○ rained.
- ◉ is raining.
- ○ The way it is

14 Ted and Mara <u>wants</u> to go to the park.
- ◉ want
- ○ wanting
- ○ The way it is

Modeled Instruction

Name

15 When the weather got cold, the leaves <u>are falling</u>.
- ○ fell.
- ○ fall.
- ○ The way it is

Tip
Ask yourself when the action is happening—now or in the past. Then choose the correct verb. Check your choice by reading the sentence to yourself with your choice in place. Let your ears tell you if it sounds correct.

16 My friend <u>kept</u> the secret.
- ○ keeping
- ○ keeped
- ● The way it is

17 Today Ms. Hill taught us why a beaver <u>build</u> dams.
- ○ are building
- ● builds
- ○ The way it is

Tip
Read the sentence to yourself to decide if there is a mistake. If you say this sentence, you will hear that you would not say *build*. What would you say?

18 The cat <u>was sleeping</u> in the sun.
- ○ sleeped
- ○ was slept
- ● The way it is

19 <u>Did you had</u> a nice time?
- ● Did you have
- ○ Do you had
- ○ The way it is

Modeled Instruction

Name _____

Modeled Instruction: Language

The next activity in this part of the test is about how sentences are put together.

Complete Sentences A sentence must have a subject and a verb. A sentence must also give a complete thought. You might see a question like this:

He lost his glove. On the bus.

The word group *On the bus* is not a sentence. It does not have a subject or a verb. It does not tell a complete thought. These two word groups could be put together to make one complete and correct sentence: *He lost his glove on the bus.*

Test-Taking Tip Look for a subject and verb in each word group. Ask yourself if the word group makes sense by itself.

Read the Sample The example word group has a subject and a verb. It also tells a complete thought. This means that it is a complete and correct sentence. The correct answer is *The way it is.*

SAMPLE
Paul is reading a funny story about dogs.

○ Paul is reading. A funny story about dogs.

○ Paul is reading a funny story. About dogs.

◉ The way it is

Modeled Instruction
21

Practice

Language

DIRECTIONS
Read the group of words in the box. Decide how they can be written to make a complete and correct sentence. If the words are already a complete and correct sentence, mark *The way it is*.

20 The balloon was popped. By a sharp thorn.

- ● The balloon was popped by a sharp thorn.
- ○ The balloon. Was popped by a sharp thorn.
- ○ The way it is

Tip
Carefully look at each word group. Does each have a person or thing that is the subject? Does each have a verb?

21 My aunt is the teacher of my best friend.

- ○ My aunt being a teacher of my best friend.
- ○ My aunt is the teacher. Of my best friend.
- ● The way it is

22 Because the bus was early. Debbie missed it.

- ○ Because the bus was early, Debbie missing it.
- ● Because the bus was early, Debbie missed it.
- ○ The way it is

Tip
Listen to each sentence. Does each give a complete thought? The first word group starts a thought but does not complete it. As you combine the sentences, be sure the verbs match.

Modeled Instruction

Name _____

23 **My dad works in a bank. Near the train station.**

- ○ My dad works in a bank near the train station.
- ○ My dad he works in a bank near the train station.
- ○ The way it is

Tip
Sometimes one word can make all the difference. You know that the second word group as it is written is not correct. Which answer choice is a correct sentence?

24 **Mom's car got dirty because of the dust on the road.**

- ○ Mom's car getting dirty because of the dust on the road.
- ○ Mom's car got dirty. Because of the dust on the road.
- ○ The way it is

Tip
Does the sentence give a complete thought? Does the verb sound right?

25 **Snow is falling. The air is cold.**

- ○ Snow is falling the air is cold
- ○ Snow is falling the air. Is cold.
- ○ The way it is

Tip
Does each sentence give a complete thought? Check your answer choices. Are they complete sentences?

Modeled Instruction

Modeled Instruction: Language

The next activity asks you questions about the way a very short story was written.

Thinking About Stories

Some questions will ask why a story was written. Some questions will ask you to choose the best last sentence of the story. Other questions will ask you to choose a sentence that does not belong in the story.

Test-Taking Tip

Before looking at the questions, make sure that you understand what the story is about. After your teacher reads the story aloud, read it again if you need to.

Read the Sample

The answer must be the best choice of an ending sentence. All the answer choices have to do with birds, but only the third choice tells about the birds at the feeder.

SAMPLE

Sally loves to watch birds at the feeder. While she eats breakfast, she watches them eat, too. Some eat seeds while others eat bits of fruit.

Which of these would go best after the last sentence?

○ Some birds come only during the winter.

○ The library has many books on birds.

○ There is always something at the feeder for every bird that comes.

Name

Practice

Language

DIRECTIONS
Read the story and the questions. Choose the best answer for each question. Mark the space for this answer.

> **Story 1**
>
> Last weekend we visited my grandmother. She always makes my favorite foods. She also tells great stories. This time we looked at old photos, too.

26 Which of these would <u>not</u> go with this story?

○ She lives in a very old house.

○ She taught me some songs from long ago.

○ She won a prize for her garden.

> **Tip**
> The word <u>not</u> is very important. You need to look for the one sentence that does not belong with the story. This story is about things a child does with a grandparent. It is not about a prize-winning garden.

27 Which would go <u>best</u> after the last sentence?

○ It was fun to see how she looked as a girl.

○ She lives about three hours away.

○ She is my dad's mother.

> **Tip**
> If you aren't sure which sentence is the best choice, try reading the story with each answer as the last sentence. This will help you figure out which makes the most sense.

Modeled Instruction

Name

Story 2

Zack was ready to go. His sleeping bag was rolled up, and his pack was full. He looked out the window waiting for his dad to get home. In a few hours, they would be on the trail.

28 Why was this story written?

- ○ To tell what to take on a trip
- ○ To tell what Zack does right before a trip
- ○ To tell where Zack and Dad were going

> **Tip**
> To answer this question, ask yourself, "What is this story about?" Then pretend that you are the writer. Ask yourself, "Why would I write this story?"

29 Which of these would go best after the last sentence?

- ○ He remembered to take his pillow.
- ○ Zack's mom said, "Did you pack your jacket?"
- ○ Zack knew this would be the best camping trip ever.

30 Which of these would not go with the story?

- ○ Every year Zack and his Dad went camping.
- ○ Zack has swimming lessons on Mondays.
- ○ It would take just a few minutes to pack the car.

> **Tip**
> Remember to look for any underlined words in the question. The underline means that this word is very important. You can try putting each sentence someplace in the story to see if it belongs. Which sentence has nothing to do with the rest of the story?

Modeled Instruction

Name _____

Modeled Instruction: Language

The last activity in this part of the test has questions about alphabetical, or ABC, order.

Alphabetical Order
Alphabetical order is a way of ordering words by using the alphabet. A word beginning with *a*, such as *apple*, would come before a word beginning with *d*, such as *dog*. You might be given three words like these:

- ○ wagon
- ◉ car
- ○ truck

You must find the word that comes first in alphbetical order. *Car* comes first because *c* comes before *t* or *w* in the alphabet

Test-Taking Tip
If you can't remember where letters come in the alphabet, look at the alphabet chart. You can also think of the alphabet song.

Look at the Sample
Look carefully at the first letter in each word. Where does each letter come in the alphabet? Since *b* comes before *c* and *p*, the answer is *basket*.

SAMPLE
- ○ pocket
- ○ circus
- ○ basket

Practice

Language

DIRECTIONS
Choose the word that comes first in alphabetical order. Mark the space in front of this word.

Modeled Instruction

27

Name _____

31.
- ○ wool
- ○ train
- ○ phone

32.
- ○ light
- ○ glass
- ○ huge

> **Tip**
> When you look at these three words, ask yourself if these words are found in the first half of the alphabet or in the second half. That will tell you in which part of the alphabet to look.

33.
- ○ floor
- ○ furniture
- ○ food

34.
- ○ coast
- ○ cry
- ○ child

> **Tip**
> All three words begin with the same first letter, *f*. This means that you will need to look at the second letter in each word.

Modeled Instruction

Name _____

Modeled Instruction: Spelling

Sight Words This part of the test asks you to find misspelled words. Some of the misspelled words are sight words. These words often have silent letters or other unusual spellings. What can you do to help you spell such a word? Close your eyes and try to see the word in your mind.

Read the Sample You may see that the underlined word *peeple* is misspelled because you have read the word *people* so many times.

SAMPLE
- ○ <u>Where</u> is my hat?
- ○ I <u>bought</u> a new bike.
- ○ We got wet <u>because</u> it rained.
- ○ Six <u>peeple</u> were late.

Practice

Spelling

DIRECTIONS
Read each sentence. Find the underlined word that is spelled wrong. Mark the space next to this sentence.

1
- ○ She is a good <u>frend</u>.
- ○ I was at <u>their</u> house.
- ○ My <u>father</u> is here.
- ○ We went <u>after</u> lunch.

> **Tip**
> Do you see a word that does not look right?

2
- ○ My mother <u>sed</u> that's okay.
- ○ <u>Their</u> coats were wet.
- ○ This cake looks <u>good</u>.
- ○ Do you <u>have</u> any?

Modeled Instruction

GO ON

Name _____

Modeled Instruction: Spelling

Spelling Consonants The sounds of consonants can blend together. If you listen carefully, you can hear the sound of each letter in words like *play*, *street*, *grape*, and *first*.

Some consonant pairs make a whole new sound, as in words like *when*, *push*, and *thin*.

Certain consonants are doubled when a word has more than one part or syllable, as in *happy*, *bubble*, and *silly*.

Read the Sample Think about the underlined word *dich*. What letters stand for the ending /sh/ sound? If you said *sh*, you are correct. This word should be spelled *dish*.

SAMPLE
- ○ Do you have a plan?
- ○ I broke a dich.
- ○ She has a pet bunny.
- ○ We can climb that tree.

Practice

Spelling

3
- ○ Last sumer was hot.
- ○ Please hurry up!
- ○ She has on a new dress.
- ○ The balloon popped.

Tip Say each two-syllable word to yourself. Which consonants need to be doubled?

4
- ○ The wind blew hard.
- ○ Dad cut the grass.
- ○ She sat very sill.
- ○ I will dry the dishes.

Tip Think about whether each underlined word makes sense in the sentence. A consonant is missing from one of the words.

Name _____

Modeled Instruction: Spelling

Spelling Vowel Sounds

A silent *e* at the end of a word can make the vowel in the middle of the word have the long sound. Say these words:

pin — pine   tap — tape   cut — cute

Long vowel sounds can have many spellings. The underlined letters in these words all stand for the long *o* sound: g<u>o</u>, r<u>o</u>p<u>e</u>, r<u>oa</u>d, sh<u>ow</u>.

The same letter combinations can often stand for different vowel sounds. Say these words:

b<u>ea</u>d — br<u>ea</u>d   b<u>oo</u>t — f<u>oo</u>t   p<u>ear</u> — h<u>ear</u> — <u>ear</u>n

Read the Sample

In these words, the letters *ore, our, or,* and *oor* are different spellings for the same vowel sound. The words *door, for,* and *pour* are all spelled correctly. So *flore* must be an incorrect spelling.

SAMPLE

○ I will mop the <u>flore</u>.   ○ This is <u>for</u> you.

○ Please answer the <u>door</u>.   ○ Please <u>pour</u> the milk.

Practice

Spelling

5 ○ The bird <u>flew</u> away.

○ I have <u>room</u> in my bag.

○ Is she in your <u>group</u>?

● I took <u>cair</u> of the cat.

6 ○ The <u>train</u> leaves at ten.

● <u>Thoes</u> books are not mine.

○ Turn on the <u>light</u>.

○ This is a <u>hard</u> problem.

> **Tip**
> Look at each underlined word. Which one does not look right? What other ways do you know to spell this vowel sound?

Modeled Instruction

Name _____

Modeled Instruction: Spelling

Spelling word endings correctly can be tricky. The test includes words that are often misspelled when endings are added.

Spelling Endings

To add an ending to a word that ends in a consonant and a y, change the y to i and add es. (*bunny/bunnies*)

To add an ending to a one-syllable word ending in a vowel and a consonant, double the last consonant. (*hop/hopping*)

If a word ends in e, drop the e when you add an ending that begins with a vowel. (*tape/taping*) If the ending starts with a consonant, keep the e. (*tape/tapes*)

To form the plural of a word ending in s, sh, ch, x, or z, add es. (*glass/glasses*)

Read the Sample

To make the word *lady* plural, you must change the y to i and add es. Therefore, you know that *ladys* is incorrectly spelled.

> **SAMPLE**
> ○ My aunt is <u>coming</u> at one.
> ○ Do you know those <u>ladys</u>?
> ○ The ball is in the <u>bushes</u>.
> ○ Mom went <u>shopping</u> for food.

Practice

Spelling

 ○ Jim is a great <u>runner</u>.
○ Ann has two <u>puppies</u>.
◉ I am <u>hopeing</u> you can come.
○ Do not sit on those <u>benches</u>.

💡 Tip
Be extra careful when adding an ending to a base word that ends in e. Remember that if a consonant comes before the e, you will need to drop the e if the ending begins with a vowel.

Modeled Instruction

Name _____

Modeled Instruction: Word Study Skills

This part of the test has questions about words. The first activity is about compound words.

Compound Words Compound words are made from two words. The compound word *raincoat* is made from the words *rain* and *coat*. In these questions, you will choose the compound word in each group.

Use the Sample Of the three words, only *birthday* is made up of two words, *birth* and *day*. You would fill in the circle under birthday.

SAMPLE A

dish   number   birthday
○   ○   ●

Practice

Word Study Skills

DIRECTIONS
Find the word that is made of two shorter words. Mark the space by your answer.

1 lower   most   grandmother
       ○   ○   ●

> **Tip**
> Don't be fooled if you see one smaller word in the big word. Even though the word *lower* has the word *low* in it, *er* is not a word.

2 roar   afternoon   school
       ○   ●   ○

3 clever   better   doghouse
       ○   ○   ●

4 brown   horseshoe   suddenly
       ○   ●   ○

Modeled Instruction

 Name

Modeled Instruction: Word Study Skills

The next activity is about word endings.

Word Endings — Read these words: *sing, sings, singing*. Each one sounds different. You know the word *sing*. You can add endings such as *s* and *ing* to make other words.

Test-Taking Tip — You need to mark the word that your teacher says. Listen carefully to the sound at the end of the word.

Use the Sample — The three words look a lot alike, but they have different endings. The ending *er* is added to *write* to make *writer*, meaning "a person who writes."

SAMPLE B

writes	writer	writing
○	●	○

Practice

Word Study Skills

DIRECTIONS
Listen as your teacher reads a word. Find the word. Mark the space under your answer.

5. runs ○   runner ○   running ●

6. player ○   played ●   playing ○

7. cleans ●   cleaning ○   cleaned ○

8. quicker ○   quickly ○   quickest ●

💡 **Tip**
Listen closely to how the word fits in the sentence you hear. Which of these sounds correct: *We player the game, We played the game,* or *We playing the game?*

Modeled Instruction

GO ON

Name _____

Modeled Instruction: Word Study Skills

The next activity is about contractions.

Contractions A contraction is a short way to write or say two words. **He'd** *like to play* means **He would** *like to play*. When a contraction is made, one or more letters are left out. An apostrophe (') takes the place of the missing letters.

Use the Sample Your teacher asked for the word that means *could not* and said the sentence *She could not finish her lunch*. Think about what *could not* means in the sentence. Choose the shortened form of the words. Any of the answer choices could fit into the sentence, but only *couldn't* does not change the meaning of the sentence.

SAMPLE C

can't couldn't wouldn't
 ○   ○   ○

Practice

Word Study Skills

DIRECTIONS
Listen as your teacher reads two words. Find the word that is a shortened form of the two words. Mark the space by your answer.

⑨   didn't   doesn't   don't
     ○   ●   ○

⑩   we're   wasn't   wouldn't
     ●   ○   ○

⑪   isn't   weren't   aren't
     ○   ●   ○

Tip
Before your teacher speaks, read the words and think what words make up each contraction. Then you will have a head start.

Tip
Look at the bits you know in the words. For example, *isn't* has *is* in it, which helps you understand that the two words are *is* and *not*.

Modeled Instruction

 Name

Modeled Instruction: Word Study Skills

The last activity is about the sounds of letters in words.

Test-Taking Tip You will do this part on your own. You will see a word that has one or two letters underlined. Say the word to yourself and see what sound or sounds the letters stand for. You will need to choose the word that has the same sound or sounds.

Use the Sample Sometimes, as here, the same sound can be spelled more than one way. *Nose* ends with the same sound that *zoo* starts with. *Nose* is the answer.

SAMPLE D

z<u>oo</u>   nose   glove   sand

Practice

Word Study Skills

DIRECTIONS
Read the word in dark print. Think about the sound that the underlined letter or letters stand for. Choose the word that has the same sound.

12 dre<u>a</u>m   bird   drive   **money**

Tip Make sure you match the sound that is underlined in the word next to the number. The *dr* sound in *dream* sounds like the *dr* in *drive*, but you are asked to match the *m* sound.

13 sm<u>i</u>le   bridge   **cry**   shirt

14 <u>s</u>torm   six   dime   **best**

Tip Remember that the sound in the answer may not always be where it is in the word in dark print.

15 <u>ch</u>air   copy   **touch**   hit

16 <u>tr</u>ain   tire   shirt   **trouble**

Tip All of these words have *t* and *r* in them, but only one sounds like the *tr* in *train*.

Modeled Instruction

Name _____

Modeled Instruction: Reading Vocabulary

This part of the test asks you to show that you understand what some words mean. The first activity is about synonyms.

Synonyms   A synonym is a word that means almost the same as another word. The word *little* means almost the same as the word *small*. They are synonyms.

Use the Sample   In this sample, think about how you use the word *tired*. The only word you would use to mean about the same thing is the word *sleepy*. The other words mean very different things. The right answer is *sleepy*. Mark the space in front of that answer choice.

SAMPLE A

If you are <u>tired</u>, you are —

○ busy   ● sleepy

○ hungry   ○ wrong

Practice

Reading Vocabulary

DIRECTIONS
Read each sentence. Find the word that means almost the same as the word that is underlined. Mark the space in front of your answer.

1 Work that is <u>easy</u> is —

○ hard   ● simple

○ yours   ○ fast

2 To <u>rush</u> is to —

○ sing   ○ stand

○ bark   ● hurry

> **Tip**
> Use the underlined word in a sentence—for example, *I will rush home*. Then put in the choices. Which word makes the most sense?

Modeled Instruction

Modeled Instruction: Reading Vocabulary

The next activity has groups of sentences. The sentences in each group show different ways of using the same word.

Multiple-Meaning Words

Many words have more than one meaning. Think about the word *row*. You can *row* a boat. You can also stand in a *row*. By reading the sentence, you can tell which kind of *row* the sentence means.

Test-Taking Tip

You will read a sentence in a box. Think about the meaning of the underlined word in the sentence. Then read the four sentences below it. Compare each sentence to the sentence in the box. Choose the sentence that uses the underlined word in the same way.

Read the Sample

Think about the meaning of *play* in the sentence in the box. It is not what you mean when you ask someone to play with you. It is not something you do in a game. Don't be fooled by the third sentence. You would *play* a part in a *play*, but only the last sentence is about acting a part. That is the correct choice.

SAMPLE B

> Janet will <u>play</u> the part of Dorothy, the main character.

In which sentence does the word <u>play</u> mean the same thing as in the sentence above?

○ Will you <u>play</u> with me after school?

○ Roy lost the chess game after a bad <u>play</u>.

○ The second-grade <u>play</u> is tomorrow.

○ Who wants to <u>play</u> the part of the dog?

Name _____

Practice

Reading Vocabulary

DIRECTIONS
Read the sentence in the box. Find the sentence that uses the word in the same way.

3 | There was a long line at the <u>bank</u>. |

In which sentence does the word <u>bank</u> mean the same thing as in the sentence above?

- ○ Chad fished from the <u>bank</u> of the river.
- ○ The snow <u>bank</u> was deep.
- ○ I can <u>bank</u> on my friend to help me.
- ● The <u>bank</u> closes at three o'clock.

> **Tip**
> In the sentence in the box, *bank* means "a place to put money." Read each sentence choice. Substitute *a place to put money* for the underlined word. Which sentence makes sense?

4 | <u>Ring</u> the bell. |

In which sentence does the word <u>ring</u> mean the same thing as in the sentence above?

- ○ Put a <u>ring</u> around the right answer.
- ● I hear the phone <u>ring</u>.
- ○ Maria put the <u>ring</u> on her finger.
- ○ Watch the clowns in the center <u>ring</u>.

> **Tip**
> How is the underlined word used? Does it show an action? Does it name a place or thing? Look at the answer choices to see which sentence uses the word in the same way.

Modeled Instruction

Name _____

Modeled Instruction: Reading Vocabulary

Context Clues The last activity in this part of the test asks you to figure out the meaning of a word in a sentence. It may be a word you do not know. The sentence will have clues that will help you pick a synonym of the word. These clues to the meaning of an unknown word are called context clues.

Read the Sample Imagine yourself using each item in the answer choices to dip out soup. A cup-shaped spoon would work best.

> **SAMPLE C**
>
> We need a <u>ladle</u> to dip out the soup. A <u>ladle</u> is a —
>
> ○ small bowl ○ napkin
> ● cup-shaped spoon ○ large fork

Practice

Reading Vocabulary

DIRECTIONS
Read each sentence. Find the word that means almost the same as the word that is underlined.

5 The sand was <u>coarse</u> and not smooth. <u>Coarse</u> means —

○ pretty ○ cold
● rough ○ brown

6 Tony is such a <u>finicky</u> eater that it is hard to fix meals for him. <u>Finicky</u> means —

○ sad ○ hungry
○ funny ● picky

Tip
Why might it be hard to fix meals for someone? Some of the answer choices have nothing to do with eating.

Modeled Instruction
40
STOP

Name

Guided Practice

Listening

DIRECTIONS
Listen as your teacher reads a sentence and then says one word from the sentence. Choose the word that means the same as the word from the sentence.

1
- ○ small
- ○ jelly
- ● huge

> **Tip**
> Think about what the word *giant* means in this sentence. You might want to picture what the sentence says. Then you can choose the word that is closest in meaning.

2
- ● middle
- ○ corner
- ○ doorway

> **Tip**
> Think about what the word *center* means in this sentence. What word comes to mind? Look at the answer choices to see if the word you thought of is one of them.

3
- ○ always
- ○ very
- ● hardly ever

4
- ○ hurt
- ● copy
- ○ hug

5
- ● give
- ○ tell
- ○ write

> **Tip**
> Which word would make sense in the sentence your teacher said?

Guided Practice

Name

DIRECTIONS
Listen to the story or paragraph. Then answer the questions.

6

> **Tip**
> When you listened to this story, you heard about what Jen and her mother planted. Mark that answer choice.

7

> **Tip**
> When you listened to this story, you heard a clue about how Jen was feeling. The story said Jen smiled when she told her mother the beans were ready to be picked.

Guided Practice

Name

8
- ○ bird
- ◉ mammal
- ○ fish

9
- ○ They have feathers.
- ○ They have claws.
- ◉ They can fly.

10
- ◉ to give directions
- ○ to give information
- ○ to tell a story

> **Tip**
> As soon as you heard the beginning of the story, "This is a way you can . . .," you got a clue as to what kind of story it is.

11
- ○ Put in toothpicks.
- ○ Cover the potato.
- ◉ Add water to the cup.

> **Tip**
> This question asks about the steps that you heard about.

12
- ○ Eating Sweet Potatoes
- ○ Planting Seeds
- ◉ Growing Plants from Vegetables

> **Tip**
> This question is another way of asking about the main idea of the story.

Guided Practice

Name

Guided Practice

Language

DIRECTIONS
Look at each sentence as your teacher reads it. Then choose the correct way to write the underlined part. If there is no mistake, choose *The way it is.*

1 Can you hear <u>me.</u>

- ○ Me!
- ● me?
- ○ The way it is

> **Tip**
> Read this sentence and ask yourself if this is a telling sentence or an asking sentence. Your answer will help you to figure out the correct ending punctuation.

2 The puppies <u>are</u> very cute.

- ○ is
- ○ was
- ● The way it is

3 <u>Were</u> sorry we missed the show.

- ○ W'ere
- ● We're
- ○ The way it is

> **Tip**
> Remember that an apostrophe is used in place of the letters that are dropped when two words are combined.

4 He was born on <u>July 1 1993.</u>

- ● July 1, 1993
- ○ july 1, 1993
- ○ The way it is

> **Tip**
> Remember that a comma is used to separate the day from the year, and the month is always capitalized.

Guided Practice
44

GO ON

Name _____

5 We went to the Beach with Dan.

- ○ Beach with dan.
- ● beach with Dan.
- ○ The way it is

> **Tip**
> Remember that only words that name a special person, place, or thing must be capitalized.

6 Last week we swim in the river.

- ● swam
- ○ swimmed
- ○ The way it is

> **Tip**
> Does the word *swim* sound correct? Since this action happened last week, the action word needs to show past time.

7 Stop! Don't walk on that thin Ice.

- ○ ice?
- ● ice!
- ○ The way it is

8 When Mr. Hill whistles, his dogs come running.

- ○ came running.
- ○ are coming running.
- ● The way it is

> **Tip**
> Look for the two verbs in this sentence. The first verb, *whistles*, tells about an action that is happening now. This helps you know that the second verb should also tell about now.

9 Yesterday we read that many bats eats insects.

- ● eat
- ○ is eating
- ○ The way it is

Guided Practice

Name

DIRECTIONS
Look at the words in the box as your teacher reads them aloud. If you see a mistake, choose the answer that makes a clear and correct sentence. If there is no mistake, choose *The way it is*.

10. The team ran. Around the field.

- ● The team ran around the field.
- ○ The team running around the field.
- ○ The way it is

Tip
Read each word group. Then ask yourself if each contains a subject and a verb.

11. Marcy sang a song during the play.

- ○ Marcy singing a song during the play.
- ○ Marcy sang a song. During the play.
- ● The way it is

Tip
Say the sentence to yourself. Does it sound right? Does it contain both a subject and a verb?

12. Mr. Jones driving a big truck.

- ○ Mr. Jones. He drives a big truck.
- ● Mr. Jones drives a big truck.
- ○ The way it is

Guided Practice

Name

DIRECTIONS
Follow along as your teacher reads each story aloud. Then choose the correct answer to each question.

Story 1

Last Friday my best friend came to my house for a sleepover. We played with puppets and put on a show for my parents. Then we made a tent out of old sheets.

13 Which of these would go best after the last sentence?

- ● Mom let us sleep in the tent.
- ○ My friend's name is Jon.
- ○ Jon gave me a puppet for my birthday.

Tip
Pay attention to any underlined words in the question. They are important. Test each answer by using it as the last sentence.

14 Why was this story written?

- ○ To tell how to make a tent
- ○ To tell about a puppet play
- ● To tell about a night of fun

Tip
To answer this question, you will need to think like a writer. Why would you write a story like this?

15 Which of these would **not** go with this story?

- ○ We used socks to make the puppets.
- ● My piano lesson is on Monday.
- ○ I was the first to fall asleep.

Guided Practice
47
GO ON

Name

Story 2

My dog Cookie is a lot of fun. This morning she jumped on my bed and took one of my socks. I chased her, but she runs faster than I do. She knows that I will chase her when she does this.

16 Which of these would <u>not</u> go with the story?

- ○ Cookie is small but very quick.
- ○ I tried to grab her but she got away.
- ◉ We also have a cat named Boots.

17 Which of these would go <u>best</u> after the last sentence?

- ○ My socks were red with black stripes.
- ○ My sister chased her, too.
- ◉ Cookie is very smart!

Tip
You know this story is about a playful dog named Cookie who likes to take things. You will look for a sentence that is <u>not</u> about this topic.

Guided Practice

Name _____

DIRECTIONS
Mark the word that comes first in alphabetical (A-B-C) order.

18 ○ point
    ○ yellow
    ○ talk

19 ○ driver
    ○ dusty
    ● dollar

20 ○ measure
    ● ladies
    ○ light

> 💡 **Tip**
> Don't be fooled when each word begins with the same letter. Just look at the second letter and ask yourself which comes first in the alphabet.

> 💡 **Tip**
> First, cover up the word that could not be correct. Then look at the words that are left.

 Name

Guided Practice

Spelling

DIRECTIONS
Read each group of sentences. Decide which underlined word is spelled wrong. Fill in the circle beside your answer.

1
○ What will <u>happen</u> next?
○ I like to <u>wear</u> red.
● That dog is very <u>littel</u>.
○ I have five <u>cents</u>.

2
● Lions are <u>wilde</u> animals.
○ <u>Once</u> I rode a horse.
○ Is my <u>face</u> clean?
○ The baby is <u>awake</u>.

> **Tip**
> Each underlined word ends with silent *e*. Which word does not need the *e*?

3
○ She lives over <u>there</u>.
○ That is a <u>thick</u> board.
● What is your <u>aje</u>?
○ My <u>father</u> works here.

> **Tip**
> Which word does not look right?

4
● That is a <u>vary</u> nice dress.
○ We went to the <u>circus</u>.
○ <u>Place</u> your feet here.
○ She has red <u>hair</u>.

> **Tip**
> Say each word to yourself. Which word has a mistake in the way the vowel sound is spelled?

5
○ That <u>pail</u> is full of water.
○ The girl <u>smiled</u> at me.
○ I need to <u>learn</u> this.
● I wrote a long <u>lettre</u>.

Guided Practice

Name _____

6
- ○ There is <u>nothing</u> here.
- ○ Turn on the <u>heet</u>.
- ○ Can you <u>throw</u> the ball?
- ○ That is a good <u>plan</u>.

> **Tip**
> Check the spelling of the vowels in these words.

7
- ○ The cat sat <u>upon</u> the bed.
- ○ That is a big <u>chair</u>.
- ○ She told a funny <u>story</u>.
- ○ The moon is very <u>brite</u>.

8
- ○ Let's go for a <u>swim</u>!
- ○ You <u>shood</u> read this.
- ○ Don't go <u>without</u> me!
- ○ We were in a <u>rush</u>.

> **Tip**
> One of these words is a sight word that you have read many times. It is not spelled the way it sounds.

9
- ○ What is Mom <u>baking</u>?
- ○ You may choose <u>first</u>.
- ○ That is the <u>sadest</u> story!
- ○ She <u>moved</u> to the city.

> **Tip**
> Sometimes when you add an ending, you must change the spelling of the base word.

10
- ○ We saw two <u>ponies</u>.
- ○ Let's go <u>skateing</u>!
- ○ Can we sit <u>closer</u> to the front?
- ○ He is <u>coming</u> over now.

Guided Practice

Name _____

Guided Practice

Word Study Skills

DIRECTIONS
Read each group of words. Find the word that has two words in it. Fill in the circle under your answer.

1   tender   darkest   basketball
     ○   ○   ●

2   tooth   snowstorm   offer
     ○   ●   ○

3   yourself   signal   notice
     ●   ○   ○

4   o'clock   daughter   paintbrush
     ○   ○   ●

> **Tip**
> Each of these words has a smaller word in it, but only one word has two smaller words in it.

DIRECTIONS
Listen as your teacher says a sentence and a word. Fill in the circle under that word.

5   talks   talked   talking
     ○   ●   ○

6   slows   slowed   slower
     ●   ○   ○

7   nicer   nicely   nicest
     ○   ●   ○

8   smarter   smartly   smartest
     ○   ○   ●

> **Tip**
> Listen closely to how the word fits in the sentence you hear.

> **Tip**
> When your teacher says each word, listen carefully to the ending.

Name _____

DIRECTIONS
Listen as your teacher reads two words and uses them in a sentence. Then choose the word that is the shortened form of the two words.

Tip: You can take each of these words apart and think of the two words used to make it.

9. that's ○　**she's** ●　he's ○
10. **you'll** ●　I'll ○　we'll ○
11. I've ○　I'll ○　**I'm** ●
12. **can't** ●　weren't ○　won't ○

DIRECTIONS
Look at the word in dark print. It has a letter or letters underlined. Then read the next three words. Find the word that has the same sound as the underlined letter or letters.

Tip: Match only the sounds that are underlined in the test word.

13. dr<u>o</u>p

    toy ○　drink ○　**box** ●

Tip: Remember that the sound in the answer may not always be where it is in the test word.

14. <u>sh</u>ake

    best ○　sand ○　**wish** ●

Tip: Make sure you match the sounds, not the letters, that are underlined in the test word.

15. <u>c</u>ity

    mouse ●　care ○　cry ○

Guided Practice

 Name

Guided Practice

Reading Vocabulary

DIRECTIONS
Choose the word that means the same, or almost the same, as the underlined word. Mark the space by your answer.

1 Twice means —
- ○ sometimes
- ○ always
- ● two times
- ○ one time

> **Tip**
> Some of the choices may be related to the underlined word but not mean the same thing.

2 A penny is the same as a —
- ○ nickel
- ○ dime
- ● cent
- ○ money

3 Something that is silly is —
- ● foolish
- ○ happy
- ○ weak
- ○ done

4 To correct is to —
- ○ color
- ● fix
- ○ choose
- ○ return

> **Tip**
> Use the underlined word in a sentence. For example, *Correct your mistake.* Then put in the choices. Which word makes the most sense?

5 Ill means —
- ○ open
- ○ gone
- ● sick
- ○ healthy

6 Something that is noisy is —
- ○ shiny
- ● loud
- ○ quiet
- ○ new

> **Tip**
> Think about the meaning of the underlined word before reading the answer choices. Then look to see if the word you thought of is one of the choices.

Guided Practice
54

Name

DIRECTIONS
Read the sentence in the box. Then read the sentences below. In which sentence does the underlined word mean the same as the underlined word in the box? Mark the space next to your answer.

7 | Your eyes and ears are part of your <u>head</u>.

In which sentence does the word <u>head</u> mean the same thing as in the above sentence?

- ○ The captain is the <u>head</u> of the team.
- ● Put a hat on your <u>head</u>.
- ○ <u>Head</u> west on Maple Street.
- ○ Rishi is at the <u>head</u> of the line.

Tip
Think about how the underlined word is used in the sentence in the box. Does it name something? Does it show an action? Does it describe something?

8 | I want to learn the <u>right</u> way to hit the ball.

In which sentence does the word <u>right</u> mean the same thing as in the sentence above?

- ○ Dad looked Ken <u>right</u> in the eye.
- ○ Your pen is <u>right</u> where you left it.
- ○ I wear my watch on my <u>right</u> hand.
- ● She did the <u>right</u> thing.

Guided Practice

Name _____

DIRECTIONS
Read the sentence. Find the word that means about the same thing as the underlined word. Mark the space next to your answer.

9 Greg saw his <u>reflection</u> when he looked in the mirror. <u>Reflection</u> means —

- ○ room
- ○ feet
- ◉ likeness
- ○ glass

10 Lynn was <u>anxious</u> for the package to arrive, unlike her sister, who was not at all interested. <u>Anxious</u> means —

- ○ sad
- ◉ eager
- ○ happy
- ○ looking

> **Tip**
> Sometimes a sentence gives you a clue by showing a contrast. Choose an answer that is the opposite of "not at all interested."

11 Sonia doesn't have a lot of money to waste, so she is a <u>thrifty</u> shopper. <u>Thrifty</u> means —

- ◉ careful
- ○ busy
- ○ poor
- ○ costly

12 Although I knew your address, it was hard to <u>locate</u> your house in the dark. <u>Locate</u> means —

- ○ lose
- ○ visit
- ○ miss
- ◉ find

> **Tip**
> Read the sentence using your answer choice in place of the word *locate*. Does it make sense?

Guided Practice

Practice Test

Listening

SAMPLE A
- ○ scare
- ● amuse
- ○ help

1
- ● every day
- ○ every week
- ○ every month

2
- ○ spill
- ○ use
- ● mix

3
- ○ whisper
- ● repeat
- ○ sing

4
- ○ warm
- ● wild
- ○ calm

5
- ○ angry
- ○ happy
- ● tired

6
- ● very big
- ○ very old
- ○ very small

7
- ○ read
- ● find
- ○ share

8
- ○ always
- ● not often
- ○ sometimes

9
- ● very
- ○ hardly
- ○ mostly

10
- ○ shook
- ● held tightly
- ○ waved

Name

SAMPLE B

SAMPLE C

11

12

13

14

Practice Test
58

GO ON

Name _____

SAMPLE D
- ○ milk
- ◉ juice
- ○ water

SAMPLE E
- ○ winter
- ○ spring
- ◉ summer
- ○ fall

15
- ○ in a park
- ◉ at a fair
- ○ in a store

16
- ◉ a booth
- ○ opposite of sit
- ○ a table

17
- ○ waffles
- ○ desserts
- ◉ ice-cream cones

18
- ○ on the beach
- ○ in the grass
- ○ in the ocean

19
- ○ a small house
- ◉ a hill in the sand
- ○ the ocean

20
- ○ 100
- ○ less than 100
- ◉ more than 100

21
- ○ how to figure skate
- ◉ about different kinds of skating
- ○ where to find an ice rink
- ○ about skating races

22
- ○ give directions
- ○ tell a story
- ◉ give information
- ○ explain how to ice skate

23
- ○ people can skate indoors
- ◉ skating is more popular than swimming
- ○ people can skate outdoors
- ○ people skate for fun

Practice Test
59

GO ON

24.
- ○ Watching Birds Eat
- ● Making a Bird Feeder
- ○ An Art Project
- ○ Using Empty Milk Cartons

25.
- ○ milk carton
- ○ scissors
- ○ string
- ● crayons

26.
- ○ hard
- ● easy
- ○ silly
- ○ long

27.
- ● put a string through the holes
- ○ tie the string onto a tree branch
- ○ cut an opening in the bottom of the carton
- ○ put in birdseed

28.
- ○ It will fall down.
- ○ You tie a string onto it.
- ● You will see birds come to eat.
- ○ You will be tired.

29.
- ○ She was hungry.
- ● She was going to bake.
- ○ She was cleaning the closet.
- ○ She was going shopping.

30.
- ○ in the sugar
- ○ on the floor
- ● on the table
- ○ next to the spoon

31.
- ○ shy
- ○ rude
- ● friendly
- ○ lazy

32.
- ○ waved to Mrs. Diaz
- ○ talked about school
- ○ left with his mother
- ● played checkers

33.
- ○ give directions
- ● Wednesday afternoons
- ○ once a month
- ○ Monday mornings

Name _____

34
- ○ a dog
- ○ a cat
- ○ a horse
- ● a pig

35
- ○ happy
- ● sad
- ○ angry
- ○ excited

36
- ○ by the Ferris wheel
- ○ by the roller coaster
- ● by the refreshment stand
- ○ by the Bingo game

37
- ○ bones
- ● muscles
- ○ heart
- ○ legs

38
- ○ 600
- ○ 50
- ○ 43
- ● 17

Practice Test

Language

SAMPLE A

Have you seen my <u>book</u>.
- ○ Book!
- ● book?
- ○ The way it is

SAMPLE B

That kitten <u>is</u> very cute.
- ○ are
- ○ were
- ● The way it is

1 Would you like a clean towel, <u>aunt Julie</u>?
- ● Aunt Julie?
- ○ Aunt Julie!
- ○ The way it is

2 The horse's coat <u>were</u> very shiny.
- ○ are
- ● was
- ○ The way it is

3 <u>Dr king, my Dentist,</u> is very nice.
- ● Dr. King, my dentist,
- ○ Dr King, my dentist,
- ○ The way it is

4 What is the <u>best</u> way to write this ending of a letter?
<u>Sincerely yours,</u>
- ○ sincerely yours,
- ○ Sincerely Yours,
- ● The way it is

5 <u>Theyre</u> all in the same class.
- ● They're
- ○ Theyr'e
- ○ The way it is

Practice Test

6 Don't jump, Tom! There is glass in the <u>grass</u>?
- ○ Grass.
- ● grass!
- ○ The way it is

7 We have music every <u>Wednesday.</u>
- ○ Wednesday?
- ○ wednesday.
- ● The way it is

8 My sister has two dogs and a <u>cat?</u>
- ● cat.
- ○ cat!
- ○ The way it is

9 My cousin <u>Tod selled</u> some cards.
- ○ tod selled
- ● Tod sold
- ○ The way it is

10 I go to <u>Carver Elementary school.</u>
- ● Carver Elementary School.
- ○ Carver Elementary school?
- ○ The way it is

11 Last year we went to <u>Chicago Illinois.</u>
- ○ chicago, illinois
- ● Chicago, Illinois.
- ○ The way it is

12 Did you know that earthquakes are very <u>dangerous.</u>
- ● dangerous?
- ○ dangerous!
- ○ The way it is

13 Please feed the cats <u>right now?</u>
- ○ Right now?
- ● right now.
- ○ The way it is

14 I went to the <u>pool with Frank.</u>
- ○ Pool with Frank.
- ○ pool with Frank?
- ● The way it is

15 It was scary when the lights <u>go</u> out.
- ● went
- ○ goed
- ○ The way it is

Practice Test
63

Name

16 "Best friends" is a great story!
- ○ "best friends"
- ◉ "Best Friends"
- ○ The way it is

17 My sister and her friend <u>are taking</u> me to a movie.
- ○ taked
- ○ is taking
- ◉ The way it is

18 Yesterday we read that the astronauts <u>studies</u> for many years.
- ◉ study
- ○ studying
- ○ The way it is

19 When my principal holds up her hand, we all <u>sat</u> down.
- ○ are sitting
- ◉ sit
- ○ The way it is

20 Last <u>Monday I wasn't</u> at practice.
- ○ monday I wasn't
- ○ Monday I wasnt
- ◉ The way it is

SAMPLE C

> The bird flew. Up in the tree.

- ○ The bird flying up in the tree.
- ● The bird flew up in the tree.
- ○ The way it is

SAMPLE D

> Nan played with her toy drum.

- ○ Nan playing with her toy drum.
- ○ Nan played. With her toy drum.
- ○ The way it is

21

> Mr. Rodgers raking the front lawn.

- ◉ Mr. Rodgers rakes the front lawn.
- ○ Mr. Rodgers. He rakes the front lawn.
- ○ The way it is

Practice Test

Name

22 Tall trees grow. In the park behind the school.

- ○ Tall trees grow in the park. Behind the school.
- ● Tall trees grow in the park behind the school.
- ○ The way it is

23 Deer were running across the empty field by the pond.

- ○ Deer running across the empty field by the pond.
- ○ Deer were running across the empty field. By the pond.
- ● The way it is

24 Her mother is a doctor at the hospital. In Oak Park.

- ● Her mother is a doctor at the hospital in Oak Park.
- ○ Her mother is a doctor. At the hospital in Oak Park.
- ○ The way it is

25 On her vacation. Judy visited many museums.

- ○ On her vacation, Judy visiting many museums.
- ● On her vacation, Judy visited many museums.
- ○ The way it is

26 Because he was careless. Jake cut his finger with the scissors.

- ● Because he was careless, Jake cut his finger with the scissors.
- ○ Because he was careless, Jake cutting his finger with the scissors.
- ○ The way it is

27 Philip drew a picture on his paper and cut it out.

- ○ Philip drew a picture on his paper. And cut it out.
- ○ Philip drawing a picture on his paper and cutting it out.
- ● The way it is

Practice Test

Name

28. Fish swim in the pond.
In front of the library.

- ○ Fish swim in the pond in front of the library.
- ○ Fish swimming in the pond in front of the library.
- ○ The way it is

29. Cindy was hurrying.
Home for dinner.

- ○ Cindy hurrying Home for dinner.
- ● Cindy was hurrying home for dinner.
- ○ The way it is

30. Ron picked up the ball.
And threw it.

- ○ Ron picking up the ball and threw it.
- ● Ron picked up the ball and threw it.
- ○ The way it is

31. The Roberts' car was dented. By a big truck.

- ○ The Roberts' car was dented by a big truck.
- ○ The Roberts' car being dented by a big truck.
- ○ The way it is

32. Sally's brother bought a computer at my dad's store.

- ○ Sally's brother he bought a computer at my dad's store.
- ○ Sally's brother bought a computer. At my dad's store.
- ● The way it is

33. The children jumped over the fence. Running around the tree.

- ○ The children jumping over the fence. They ran around the tree.
- ● The children jumped over the fence and ran around the tree.
- ○ The way it is

Practice Test

Name _____

SAMPLE

Not all apples are alike. Apples come in different sizes, colors, and flavors. Some apples are good for eating. Other apples are best for baking.

E Which of these would go best after the last sentence?

○ Ann's uncle has a big apple tree beside his house.

○ An apple makes a great after-school snack.

● Next time you buy apples, look at all the different kinds!

F Why was this story written?

○ To tell how to grow apples

◐ To tell about types of apples

○ To tell how to make an apple pie

Story 1

Riding my bike to school, I waved to our neighbor out in her yard. She was digging in her flower bed. She had many pots of colorful flowers lined up on her lawn. After school, I saw her standing by the fence.

34 Which of these would go **best** after the last sentence?

◐ She was looking at the beautiful garden she had planted.

○ When she is on vacation, I mow her lawn.

○ Some flowers grow better in sun than in the shade.

35 Which of these would <u>not</u> go with this story?

○ Her name is Mrs. Henry, and she is my mom's friend.

○ She had a shovel, a hoe, and a long hose.

◐ A store that sells plants is called a nursery.

Practice Test

Story 2

Polly loves to make things for presents. Last year she made some refrigerator magnets to give her mom for Mother's Day. She drew a picture of each person in the family. Then she cut it out and pasted it to a jar lid. On the back of the lid, she glued a small magnet.

36 **Which of these would go best after the last sentence?**

- ○ She used markers to draw her pictures.
- ● Her mom loves this gift and uses the magnets every day.
- ○ It's important to keep some foods in the refrigerator.

37 **Which of these would not go with the story?**

- ○ Polly often gets good gift ideas from library books.
- ○ Polly spends time instead of money on her gifts.
- ● Polly wants to learn how to dance.

38 **Why was this story written?**

- ● To tell about one of Polly's gifts
- ○ To tell about Mother's Day
- ○ To tell why people like Polly's presents

Story 3

José stopped in front of the pen. A white puppy came up to the wire mesh. The puppy wagged its tail and tried to lick José's fingers. Then he gave a friendly bark and began to chase his tail. "His name is Snowball," said Mr. West. "Looks like he's picked you out!"

39 Why was this story written?

- ○ To tell about a cute puppy
- ○ To tell why José wants a puppy
- ○ To tell about how to pick a puppy

40 Which of these would go **best** after the last sentence?

- ● Snowball was the puppy that José took home.
- ○ José also looked at kittens and birds.
- ○ José said, "I want to look at the other puppies."

41 Which of these would **not** go with this story?

- ○ José had been promised a puppy for his birthday.
- ● The cats made José sneeze.
- ○ The puppy had curly hair and floppy ears.

Practice Test

Name

Story 4

My brother Ben is building a sailboat in his free time. He bought a kit that has all the parts. My Aunt Susan is helping him on weekends. She has built several boats just like Ben's.

42 Which of these would go <u>best</u> after the last sentence?
- ○ Aunt Susan says she will teach me to sail.
- ○ Ben began working on the boat last month.
- ● Ben says they make a great team.

43 Why was this story written?
- ○ To tell why Ben likes to sa
- ● To tell about Ben's special project
- ○ To tell how to sail a boat

SAMPLE G
- ○ inch
- ○ know
- ● hawk

44
- ○ table
- ● seahorse
- ○ umbrella

45
- ○ city
- ● chore
- ○ close

46
- ○ mild
- ○ price
- ● medicine

47
- ○ nurse
- ● lift
- ○ mail

Practice Test

Spelling

SAMPLE

- ○ Nate is an only <u>child</u>.
- ○ The cat sat in the <u>window</u>.
- ● The <u>croud</u> clapped.
- ○ He wore a <u>black</u> hat.

1
- ○ Where is my <u>sock</u>?
- ● I'm in second <u>grad</u>.
- ○ Jan hurt her <u>elbow</u>.
- ○ Lester wants a new <u>car</u>.

2
- ○ I love apple <u>pie</u>.
- ○ The <u>grass</u> is quite green.
- ● <u>Wonce</u> we lived here.
- ○ Do you know this <u>song</u>?

3
- ○ <u>Those</u> pencils are mine.
- ○ The cows are in the <u>barn</u>.
- ○ Bananas come in a <u>bunch</u>.
- ● This is not <u>az</u> I left it!

4
- ○ Wipe up that <u>spill</u>.
- ● Pat has a <u>wite</u> kitten.
- ○ Sue lost her <u>ring</u>.
- ○ He broke a <u>dish</u>.

5
- ○ There is <u>one</u> cookie left.
- ○ The <u>rocket</u> flew very high.
- ○ It began to <u>rain</u>.
- ● They love <u>raceing</u> their bikes.

6
- ○ When does baseball <u>season</u> begin?
- ● She has on a red <u>skert</u>.
- ○ Babies have small <u>feet</u>.
- ○ She has read <u>less</u> than I.

7
- ○ Please <u>mail</u> this letter.
- ○ Carefully <u>chew</u> each bite.
- ● He has one older <u>brothir</u>.
- ○ Who made this <u>mark</u>?

8
- ○ Do you want any more <u>peas</u>?
- ○ Ann is <u>running</u> in a race.
- ○ She will be <u>eight</u> tomorrow.
- ● Will you teach me that <u>trik</u>?

9
- ○ Honey is very <u>sweet</u>.
- ● My favorite color is <u>blu</u>.
- ○ We heard a loud <u>bang</u>.
- ○ Just <u>aim</u> at the target.

Practice Test

Name

10
- ● They stud in line.
- ○ She sat behind Felix.
- ○ Where does this trail go?
- ○ The red towel is mine!

11
- ● I joust caught the bus.
- ○ Mom chopped down the tree.
- ○ They jumped rope.
- ○ I put the blocks away.

12
- ○ We will leave at ten.
- ○ Is that the tallest tree?
- ○ He blew his whistle.
- ● Mom went to the stor.

13
- ○ I missed my friend.
- ● That toy car is missing a weel.
- ○ Which way is east?
- ○ Tomorrow is Friday.

14
- ○ I can't wait for you.
- ○ That team beat us!
- ● Mayby we will have music.
- ○ Joe leaned against the wall.

15
- ○ This button is loose.
- ○ We gave the dog a bath.
- ○ The books are in the bookcase.
- ● She read us a great storey.

16
- ● She goze to my school.
- ○ The town is beyond those hills.
- ○ A blue whale is huge.
- ○ His hands were shaking.

17
- ● Why are you in such a ruch?
- ○ He lives in a big town.
- ○ Is that dog mean?
- ○ I ate both cookies.

18
- ○ Stand by the wall.
- ● The horse got luse.
- ○ I read while I waited.
- ○ Luis is baking a pie.

19
- ○ Let's go shopping!
- ○ This is my bag.
- ● That stown is so smooth.
- ○ Why are you here?

Practice Test

GO ON

Name _____

20
- ● We played at the parck.
- ○ Did you see that rabbit?
- ○ Let's go to the zoo.
- ○ I saw her again last night.

21
- ○ The bird hurt its wing.
- ○ The sky looked gray.
- ○ The twins look alike.
- ● I will ster the soup.

22
- ○ Is that a good book?
- ○ Look behind the door.
- ● I pade for lunch.
- ○ Please stop shoving!

23
- ○ Did you thank her?
- ● We have too dogs.
- ○ That girl likes cats.
- ○ She never stops rushing.

24
- ○ The cat is hiding.
- ○ She sat in a chair.
- ○ Are you awake?
- ● It is verry hot.

25
- ● Jason droped the ball.
- ○ Give me a chance.
- ○ Let's go swimming.
- ○ Did you write this story?

26
- ○ He is the dog's owner.
- ● Have some frea popcorn!
- ○ I wrote her a long letter.
- ○ I lost a tooth.

27
- ● We learnd about rocks.
- ○ My hat is made of wool.
- ○ Sally lost one mitten.
- ○ Look between the posts.

28
- ○ When does school start?
- ○ The baby is asleep.
- ● He is a nise dog.
- ○ What page are we on?

29
- ○ We sat in a circle.
- ○ It will snow tonight.
- ○ Mom looked under the hood.
- ● That is a tall ladir.

30
- ○ That cat is very shy.
- ● Sumtimes it snows in May.
- ○ Let's eat at noon.
- ○ The birds began to chirp.

Practice Test
73

Name _____

Word Study Skills

SAMPLE A
player ○ sunshine ○ uncover ○

SAMPLE C
hasn't ○ haven't ○ wasn't ○

1. bookmark ○ even ○ heart ○
2. women ○ weekend ○ remain ○
3. farmer ○ birdhouse ○ stopped ○
4. direction ○ across ○ myself ○

9. we've ○ you've ○ I've ○
10. he's ○ she's ○ that's ○
11. we'll ○ I'll ○ she'll ○
12. isn't ○ doesn't ○ wouldn't ○

SAMPLE B
sweeter ○ sweetly ○ sweetest ○

SAMPLE D
j<u>e</u>t
sing ○ gate ○ edge ○

5. brushed ○ brushes ○ brushing ○
6. covers ○ covered ○ covering ○
7. builds ○ builder ○ building ○
8. shorter ○ shortly ○ shortest ○

13. <u>n</u>ail
    bell ○ know ○ far ○
14. <u>e</u>very
    use ○ bear ○ guess ○
15. me<u>lt</u>
    black ○ fault ○ tail ○
16. n<u>o</u>se
    boat ○ lose ○ out ○

Practice Test
74

GO ON →

Name _____

17. toot**h**
- table ○
- thirteen ●
- house ○

18. toy
- noise ●
- stop ○
- rose ○

19. mak**e**
- mice ○
- count ●
- knife ○

20. mea**n**
- bear ○
- tree ●
- head ○

21. sh**ip**
- best ○
- chair ○
- machine ●

22. loo**k**
- could ●
- hole ○
- rub ○

23. st**ick**
- sad ○
- thirsty ●
- older ○

24. wh**ere**
- whisper ●
- toss ○
- chop ○

25. cou**nt**
- cup ○
- flower ●
- told ○

26. bring
- song ●
- range ○
- good ○

27. blow
- smoke ●
- enjoy ○
- crown ○

28. ma**tch**
- flag ●
- said ○
- yawn ○

29. st**rong**
- sting ○
- strip ●
- track ○

30. bi**rd**
- hair ○
- were ●
- torn ○

31. mi**le**
- chin ○
- fly ●
- trail ○

32. chain
- bench ●
- frog ○
- cage ○

Practice Test
75

 Name

Reading Vocabulary

SAMPLE A

A <u>tale</u> is a kind of —
- ○ toy
- ● story
- ○ game
- ○ picture

1 To <u>start</u> is to —
- ○ end
- ○ leave
- ● begin
- ○ break

2 <u>Finished</u> means —
- ○ placed
- ● done
- ○ gone
- ○ fixed

3 To <u>ask</u> is to —
- ● question
- ○ answer
- ○ write
- ○ buy

4 A <u>piece</u> of a puzzle is a —
- ○ game
- ○ book
- ○ plate
- ● part

5 Something that is <u>quick</u> is —
- ○ slow
- ○ easy
- ● fast
- ○ clear

6 <u>Loud</u> means —
- ● noisy
- ○ happy
- ○ lonely
- ○ new

7 <u>Uneasy</u> means not —
- ○ hard
- ● comfortable
- ○ alone
- ○ able

8 To <u>rush</u> is to —
- ○ wait
- ○ run
- ○ swim
- ● hurry

9 A <u>city</u> is most like a —
- ○ park
- ○ garden
- ● town
- ○ building

10 Something that is <u>below</u> is —
- ○ far
- ○ above
- ○ high
- ● under

11 To <u>turn</u> is to —
- ○ move slowly
- ○ go straight
- ○ go fast
- ● move around

12 The <u>center</u> is the —
- ○ edge
- ● middle
- ○ side
- ○ circle

Practice Test

Name _____

SAMPLE B

Will you be ready to <u>leave</u> at 3 o'clock?

In which sentence does the word <u>leave</u> mean the same thing as in the sentence above?

- ○ Dad took a <u>leave</u> from his job.
- ○ <u>Leave</u> the book on the table.
- ○ Don't <u>leave</u> out any answers.
- ◉ We <u>leave</u> on our trip tomorrow.

13 I have been living here for a <u>short</u> time.

In which sentence does the word <u>short</u> mean the same thing as in the sentence above?

- ○ Grandpa is a <u>short</u> man.
- ○ The car stopped <u>short</u> at the corner.
- ◉ The path is <u>short</u>.
- ○ Kevin was <u>short</u> with me when I asked him a question.

14 Maggie hurt her <u>foot</u> when she fell.

In which sentence does the word <u>foot</u> mean the same thing as in the sentence above?

- ○ One <u>foot</u> is the same as 12 inches.
- ◉ For how long can you hop on one <u>foot</u>?
- ○ Who will <u>foot</u> the bill for the party?
- ○ We met at the <u>foot</u> of the hill.

15 Are things going <u>well</u> at school?

In which sentence does the word <u>well</u> mean the same thing as in the sentence above?

- ○ I know my lines in the play <u>well</u>.
- ○ <u>Well</u>, I don't know the answer.
- ○ Jan is not <u>well</u>.
- ◉ The work was done <u>well</u>.

Name

16

> I want to <u>show</u> you my new toy.

In which sentence does the word <u>show</u> mean the same thing as in the sentence above?

- ● <u>Show</u> me your answer.
- ○ Will you <u>show</u> me how to do the problem?
- ○ Liz likes to <u>show</u> off her new clothes.
- ○ Our class put on a puppet <u>show</u>.

SAMPLE C

As the storm <u>approached</u>, the sky grew darker. <u>Approached</u> means —

- ○ went away
- ○ rained
- ○ blew
- ● came nearer

17 Pam didn't want anything too unusual, so she chose an <u>ordinary</u> hat. <u>Ordinary</u> means —

- ● plain
- ○ fancy
- ○ old
- ○ order

18 We bought flowers from the <u>peddler</u> who had a cart on the street corner. A <u>peddler</u> is someone who —

- ○ grows flowers
- ● sells things
- ○ plants things
- ○ rides a bicycle

19 "I really want to go on this trip," said Ramon. "I will <u>plead</u> with my parents to let me go." <u>Plead</u> means —

- ○ ask
- ○ answer
- ● beg
- ○ tell

20 The speaker made a <u>gesture</u> with his hands to help get across his idea. A <u>gesture</u> is a —

- ○ clap
- ● movement
- ○ word
- ○ noise

21 Ms. Blank said we could write a report or give an <u>oral</u> report to the class. <u>Oral</u> means —

- ○ short
- ○ long
- ○ interesting
- ● spoken

22 We looked down at the river from the <u>peak</u> of the mountain. <u>Peak</u> means —

- ● top
- ○ bottom
- ○ middle
- ○ snow

Practice Test